AF491250

LIMITATIONS AND LOSSES

Limitations and
Losses

TWO INESCAPABLE
REALITIES

---

the serial intellectual

Innovative Industries 1, LLC

Copyright © 2024 by the serial intellectual

All rights reserved. No part of this book may be reproduced in any manner whatsoever without written permission except in the case of brief quotations embodied in critical articles and reviews.

First Printing, 2024

Contents

1

Introduction

Why did I write this book? My age! I'm fifty-six years old. At this age, limitations and losses become undeniably prevalent and apparent, almost impossible to escape or ignore. While they may have their seasons, they tend to intensify as we age and we become increasingly self-aware of their presence in our lives. Therefore, I've embarked on writing this book because they consistently confront me virtually every day and moment.

The second reason for addressing limitations and losses in this book relates to my heightened awareness of personal inadequacies, failures, and the accompanying frustrations. Like many, I haven't always handled losses in the most constructive manner. In various seasons and periods of my life, I encountered loss and, regrettably, responded with poor decisions rather than choosing the right course. Instead of persevering, I opted to escape and made choices that proved to be detrimental. It became evident to me that these decisions, made in the midst of adversity, served as vivid examples of my own limitations. I possessed the willingness and desire, but I often lacked the capacity to align my actions with my intentions. As I progressed through life, growing increasingly aware of my limitations, it gave rise to a considerable amount of frustration. Reflecting on my failures, there were moments when this frustration even turned into anger.

Although it cannot be used as an excuse, this realization has consistently served as a valid explanation and a means for me to move forward without becoming mired in my limitations and losses, preventing further self-destruction. In the past, I have endured numerous painful losses that, in a way, partnered with my limitations to unveil a part of my identity that I had been reluctant to confront. I've always held the belief that, with the right opportunities and sufficient discipline, I could overcome challenges and obstacles. Furthermore, I've fancied myself as a person who would never intentionally harm anyone. However, as I previously mentioned, this idealized self-image has been shattered on occasion, and I've encountered these two formidable adversaries, limitations, and losses, waiting to be acknowledged in the midst of those moments.

The third motivation behind writing this book stems from my experiences supporting friends and family as they navigate their own seasons of limitations and losses. Few things are as agonizing as witnessing the suffering of those you hold dear, especially when they are unable to alleviate their own hardships. What can be even more exasperating is when you attempt to assist them and come to the realization that your own abilities are limited. When someone you love experiences loss, it affects you deeply. Their pain becomes your pain, and their joy becomes your joy. However, when they weep, you, too, share in their sorrow. Thus, I embark on this writing journey because within my soul resides a place filled with both frustration and pain, largely due to the countless limitations and losses I have witnessed among my loved ones and friends.

The fourth rationale behind my decision to write this book arises from my experiences within one of America's largest cities, Baltimore, spanning well over a decade. During this time, I observed numerous organizations and thousands of well-intentioned, highly skilled, and resourceful individuals strategically collaborating to address and rectify various vices, social inequalities, and injustices prevalent in the city. Despite these efforts, substantial macrolevel changes remained elusive.

It became evident to me that we were contending with sociological limitations and losses.

I recognized that cities like Baltimore suffer from a sociological autoimmune ailment where the collective endeavors of well-meaning individuals striving to enhance the city are often met with resistance and opposition instead of cooperation to foster improvement. My own frustrations, as well as those of others directly grappling with their limitations and losses, prompted me to delve into this issue. While we cannot enumerate all of Baltimore's losses here, it is worth noting the city's long standing struggle with gun violence, resulting in the loss of countless lives—well over three hundred per year for an extended period. This figure doesn't even encompass the lives forever altered by disabilities stemming from gun-related trauma, rendering individuals unable to return to work, among other life-altering consequences. Baltimore, a city of beauty and potential, is also marred by its profound limitations and losses. These realities have served as a powerful source of inspiration for me to address the issue of limitations and losses.

The final reason to write is the shared need for assistance in navigating the complexities of limitations and losses. It is my firm belief that both you and I grapple with these challenges in our lives. To continue my journey of holistic exploration and constructive management of these issues, I have turned to research, learning, and writing as invaluable tools. Through substantial contemplation, strategic planning, writing endeavors, collaborative efforts, and dialogues with various individuals, I have acquired a wealth of insights. I am eager to impart these lessons to you because I understand that, much like myself, you constantly confront limitations and losses. Some of you may find yourselves in unique seasons characterized by these challenges, facing desperate times and grappling with feelings of isolation, uncertainty, desperation, frustration, dismay, and disillusionment. I want you to know that I have traversed similar paths, as have countless others. Therefore, I write with the purpose of offering encouragement, education, and empowerment. My hope is that, together, we can deepen our understanding of limitations and losses and collaboratively discover healthier and more holistic methods for managing them.

The word "limitations" has its origins in the Latin language. It can be traced back to the Latin word "limitatio," which is derived from "limitare," meaning "to limit" or "to set a boundary." "Limitation" has been in use in the English language for centuries and has retained its essential meaning of denoting boundaries, constraints, or restrictions throughout its linguistic history. In the context of research or studies, limitations are the inherent weaknesses, shortcomings, or factors that may affect the reliability, validity, or generalizability of the findings. These limitations are acknowledged to provide a transparent assessment of the study's boundaries. In technology and innovation, limitations represent the technical, practical, or resource-based constraints that affect the development, functionality, or performance of a product, system, or process. When discussing personal growth and development, limitations refer to self-imposed or external obstacles that hinder an individual's progress or potential for self-improvement.

The word "losses" has its origin in Old English. It can be traced back to the Old English word "los," which means "destruction" or "perishing." Overtime, the word evolved and retained its essential meaning of referring to the negative outcomes or reductions in value or well-being that occur when something valuable is diminished or no longer available. Emotional losses pertain to the feelings of grief, sadness, or sorrow that individuals experience when they lose someone or something dear to them, such as a loved one or a cherished possession. In a business context, losses typically refer to negative financial results where expenses exceed revenues, resulting in a net loss. This can also include losses due to theft, fraud, or asset damage. In physics, losses typically refer to reducing energy or power in a system due to various factors like friction, resistance, or inefficiencies in energy transfer. In sports, losses are recorded when a team or individual does not win a game or match. It represents a failure to secure a victory.

Limitations are constraints or boundaries that delineate the scope of possibility and permissibility, whether inherent or deliberate, without inherently bearing a negative connotation and frequently serving purposes like safety or fairness, whereas losses involve the absence or diminishment of something valuable or significant, usually encompassing negative events or outcomes, necessitating adaptation or recovery, and often arising unexpectedly or unintentionally within the intricate fabric of human experiences.

LIMITATIONS
LOSSES

2

Chapter 2: THE RELATIONSHIP BETWEEN LIMITATIONS AND LOSSES

The relationship between limitations and losses is undeniably intertwined. They are constant companions, inevitably appearing together in all situations. Although their intensity may vary, they consistently coexist. When we encounter a limitation, we concurrently experience a degree of loss. Likewise, when we face a loss, we also confront some form of limitation, particularly regarding our ability to mitigate that loss. To effectively handle them in a comprehensive and healthy manner, and to embrace them as companions that offer encouragement and character growth, we must recognize their presence together in every circumstance.

It's apparent that many individuals place a greater emphasis on losses compared to limitations. This tendency is quite natural, as limitations often become a part of our daily lives, and we subconsciously learn to manage and adapt to them. On the other hand, losses tend to evoke more profound emotions, such as grief, arising from events like death, the end of a relationship, relocation, or financial setbacks from bank accounts or investments. Socially and culturally, we tend to give more attention to losses than limitations. Nevertheless, it's crucial to recognize that they are invariably intertwined. Regardless of cultural or temporal influences that might prioritize one over the other, limitations and losses consistently coexist.

How do they work together?

Limitations, in essence, establish a cap on our abilities, prompting us to look beyond this imposed boundary. This exploration beyond the cap reveals the gap between our limitations and the potential we could achieve without it. The extent of this gap, the difference between our limitations and our untapped potential, is measured in terms of loss. This is how limitations and losses interplay. Conversely, when we encounter a loss, whether it's in the form of an emotional, physical, relational, or material loss, our immediate response often involves pondering how we could have prevented it. We may question the reasons behind the loss, seeking a way to rectify it. However, in cases where losses occur without clear answers to the "why" or where understanding the "why" would only delay the inevitable, we are confronted with limitations. So, these two elements work in tandem, with their significance varying based on the nature of our experiences.

Illustrations are one of the most effective tools for helping us to understand things. Let's look at a few historical events that will give us more clarity on the issue of limitations and losses. The first illustrative event to examine is the September 11, 2001, terrorist attacks in the US. While this event is well known globally, it's important to highlight the role of limitations and losses associated with it. First, let's focus on the losses, which are more readily apparent. The losses are conspicuous, including the tragic loss of life, the temporary disruption of travel, job losses, economic repercussions, and the subsequent loss of lives as the

US engaged in wars with other nations, leading to casualties among soldiers and those they waged war with. Husbands, fathers, brothers, sisters, and mothers lost their lives, resulting in a profound sense of loss. Even though the US has since withdrawn from Afghanistan, the enduring effects of these events persist to this day.

Over twenty years later, we continue to endure losses stemming from these events. Many of my readers are still grappling with the loss of loved ones, friends, jobs, and some even bear the burden of disabilities—whether they are mental, emotional, or related to PTSD—resulting from the aftermath of these events. While the losses are readily apparent, it's equally crucial to consider the limitations. To gain insight into how this tragedy unfolded and how such a catastrophic event could occur, we must examine the limitations. How did it happen? How did individuals hijack four planes, crash them into buildings, and fundamentally transform American culture, leading to the loss of thousands of lives and serving as a primary catalyst for war and numerous other consequences?

Upon reflecting on and analyzing the event, we encounter limitations in the form of catastrophic failures within our systems. The systems that were meant to prevent certain individuals from causing harm faltered. Prior to 9/11, it was customary for flights to operate with the cockpit door wide open. This practice allowed passengers to see inside because hijackings were exceedingly rare, especially within the US The notion of someone hijacking a plane and intentionally crashing it into a building was inconceivable. Consequently, the limitations of our security systems failed to protect us on that fateful day.

In response, the aviation industry introduced measures like reinforced cockpit doors and heightened security protocols at airports to address these limitations. These include longer lines, the introduction of baggage and body scanning machines, as well as stringent restrictions on items allowed on planes. While these measures are implemented for security purposes, they impose limitations on travelers. In this context, limitations arise due to the need to address security concerns stemming from the 9/11 attacks. Upon further analysis, it becomes evident that certain governmental departments failed to communicate and collaborate effectively, as they didn't perceive a strong necessity to do so.

Failures and limitations were apparent everywhere, making it clear that the systems in place at the time were insufficient to protect America from such a tragic event as 9/11. Examining how limitations and losses intertwined in this context could provide valuable insights, but there are more real-life examples to explore. A more recent and globally relevant example is the COVID-19 pandemic. As the virus spread and people fell ill, governments worldwide responded differently. The immediate concern was the loss of life, which alarmed not only the world but also scientists, virologists, and governments.

Efforts were made to address this through measures like lockdowns, mask mandates, and the development of vaccines to mitigate the impact of COVID-19. However, in dealing with the pandemic, both limitations and losses were experienced. Initially, there was hope that the right vaccines might confer immunity, but it became evident that this was not the case. Many vaccinated individuals still fell seriously ill, especially if they had underlying health conditions, highlighting the limitations of the vaccines and the losses incurred.

The limitations of measures such as masking and maintaining six feet distance became evident as they didn't work as effectively as expected in controlling the spread of the virus. It was a stark confrontation with our inability to halt the virus's transmission. At the same time, we were grappling with losses, including not only the tragic loss of lives but also the economic consequences of the pandemic. Many businesses had to close, leading to job losses, highlighting the intricate connection between limitations and losses in both the context of the COVID-19 pandemic and the 9/11 events.

3

Chapter 3: ILLUSTRATIONS OF LIMITATIONS AND LOSSES

Technology

Technology indeed has a significant role in overcoming limitations, but it can also introduce new limitations. For instance, much of today's work and activities have shifted online and become internet dependent. However, when we encounter power outages or internet disruptions, we are suddenly faced with limitations.

Moreover, technology not only alleviates limitations but also introduces new ones. Jobs are being lost due to technological advancements as manufacturing processes are increasingly automated. In retail stores, self-checkout systems and facial recognition technologies are being implemented, reducing the need for human attendants. These technological changes lead to job losses and highlight the coexistence of limitations and losses in the realm of technology.

Acknowledging the advantages of technology, we must remain aware that it also introduces limitations and losses into our lives. For instance, the distressing experience of losing a debit card can severely impede our ability to function in various life domains. This situation is reminiscent of earlier times when we carried physical cash in wallets, risking loss. In the modern era, the loss of a debit card prompts us to contact the bank for card cancellation and replacement, or we visit the bank for a temporary card. A technological solution to address this issue involves loading our card information onto our smartphones.

In the realm of technology, we continually strive to adapt to limitations and cope with losses. I recommend technology as a domain to explore if you wish to gain insights into how limitations and losses manifest, as well as observe the various methods people employ to address them. This field provides a clear and illustrative perspective on these dynamics.

Healthcare

Healthcare, whether viewed through the lens of societal health systems or individual patient care, reveals a shared landscape characterized by distinct attributes. Within this intricate domain, we inevitably encounter the stark reality of limitations that affect our approach to various medical conditions and diseases. Some afflictions continue to defy our best efforts, lacking effective treatments or eluding the discovery of a cure. In such challenging cases, our capacity to provide comprehensive solutions is constrained, and healthcare professionals often find themselves offering palliative support and encouragement, emphasizing comfort and quality of life in the face of the condition's unyielding nature.

Even in the presence of the most cutting-edge medical technology and advancements, the specter of loss remains a palpable presence in the realm of healthcare. These losses can manifest in various forms, from the loss of sensory perceptions like vision or hearing to the loss of a limb or a once-familiar ability. These are poignant reminders that healthcare, for all its promise and potential, carries inherent limitations and is marked by the enduring presence of losses. The ultimate and universally acknowledged loss in healthcare is, of course, the loss of life itself. Many readers may have personal experiences of bearing witness to the suffering of a loved one or friend despite the valiant efforts of medical professionals and the advancements of modern medicine. In this context, healthcare stands as a domain where both the stark realities of limitations and the profound weight of losses are brought to the forefront.

Yet, within this intricate landscape, healthcare also embodies a narrative of progress and resilience, a testament to the indomitable human spirit in the face of adversity. Never before in the annals of history have we possessed such extensive capabilities for treating diseases, saving lives, and aiding the recovery of patients. The relentless pursuit of scientific discovery and technological innovation has expanded the boundaries of what is possible in healthcare. These achievements have transformed it into a realm where we are more adept than ever at mitigating losses and circumventing certain limitations, offering hope and healing to those in need.

Nonetheless, the healthcare sector remains an instructive and humbling domain for comprehending the dichotomy of limitations and losses. It offers a profound lesson in the recognition of human vulnerability and the impermanence of life. It underscores the importance of cherishing each moment and valuing the small victories in the face of adversity. In the end, it is a testament to the resilience of the human spirit, the relentless pursuit of progress, and the enduring commitment to alleviating suffering and improving the human condition.

Law

Laws wield the power to hold individuals accountable for their actions when they inflict harm, but their reach falls short when it comes to preventing harm in the first place. In essence, laws are the structural backbone of a functioning society, designed to establish order and foster safety among its members. However, a universal truth prevails: laws are often transgressed, revealing their inherent limitations.

A poignant example of this limitation is the prevalence of laws prohibiting homicide in nearly every nation, yet this very law is frequently violated. It's clear that while the law operates as a framework that encourages compliance and instills fear in some individuals, thereby deterring them from committing unlawful acts, it doesn't manage to dissuade everyone. The effectiveness of laws, it seems, varies across the board, with some being remarkably successful while others fall short of their intended goals.

In a paradoxical twist, laws themselves can sometimes become agents of loss. A prime illustration can be found in the domain of tax laws. The mere mention of taxes often invokes thoughts of financial loss in the minds of many. Exceptions to this rule are few and far between, usually residing among the less than 1 percent of individuals who have amassed substantial wealth and possess the knowledge and resources to effectively minimize their tax liability. These exceptions aside, tax laws are largely associated with financial detriment for the majority of citizens.

In essence, the law is a multifaceted tool in our societal arsenal. It holds wrongdoers accountable, strives to create order, and promotes safety. However, it can't always avert harm, and its effectiveness can vary widely. Furthermore, the very laws meant to protect can inadvertently bring about losses for those subject to them. This complex relationship between law and society highlights the intricate dance between rules, enforcement, and their real-world impact.

Justice System

The justice system, tasked with the formidable responsibility of administering the law and upholding the principles of fairness and justice, is a complex and multifaceted institution that, like any human endeavor, is not without its limitations and losses. When we scrutinize this vital system, we inevitably encounter the stark reality of constraints and imperfections that shape its operation.

One fundamental limitation that becomes evident in the realm of justice is its ability to apprehend wrongdoers and, subsequently, its capacity to accurately determine guilt or innocence. While the system strives to seek the truth, it is not immune to errors and the challenges inherent in investigations, evidence gathering, and the complexities of the human psyche. Instances of wrongful convictions, where innocent individuals find themselves ensnared in the justice system's web, serve as sobering reminders of these limitations. The realization that justice, despite its noble pursuit of truth and fairness, is fallible in its judgments represents a significant loss, not only for the individuals directly affected but also for society as a whole.

Another dimension in which the justice system exhibits limitations is its propensity for inequity. It occasionally imposes disproportionately severe punishments for certain crimes or misdemeanors, contributing to a sense of imbalance within society. The differential treatment of individuals based on factors like race, socioeconomic status, or access to legal representation further underscores the system's imperfections. This inequity is not only a limitation but also a profound loss, particularly for those who bear the brunt of harsh sentences or discriminatory practices.

Yet, it's important to acknowledge that the justice system is not a monolithic entity, and within its complexities, it also embodies resilience and adaptability. Over the course of history, the system has evolved, with reforms implemented to address some of its limitations and correct its injustices. Legal professionals, activists, and policymakers have tirelessly worked to introduce changes that promote a fairer and more equitable system.

In essence, the justice system serves as a sobering reminder of the intricate interplay between limitations and losses in the quest for justice and the administration of the law. While it reflects the human capacity for error and the potential for inequity, it also highlights the ongoing commitment to improve, reform, and enhance its functioning. Through awareness, advocacy, and a collective determination to uphold the principles of fairness and justice, society continues to grapple with these limitations, transforming them into catalysts for positive change and the pursuit of a more just legal system.

Relationships

Limitations and losses are also evident in the context of relationships. Despite our aspirations for healthy, loving, and thriving relationships, we must acknowledge that we each carry our imperfections, personal limitations, and past experiences into every relationship. The individuals we interact with similarly possess their own limitations and past losses that have shaped them. These unique qualities intersect within the relationship, leading to experiences of limitations and losses. It's essential to recognize that sometimes the challenges in a relationship are rooted in limitations rather than ill intent or deliberate harm.

Limitations typically stem from past wounds and injuries, manifesting as hindrances that restrict our capacity to love, relate, listen, learn, and grow. This pattern is evident across various types of relationships, including family, marriage, parent-child, work, and friendship. In all these relationship dynamics, limitations and losses become apparent. One of the most agonizing experiences in relationships is the loss of a loved one, not just due to circumstances like death but also because of conflicts, disagreements, and emotional hurt. The ensuing pain, discomfort, and disgust often lead to separation and parting ways.

In some cases, such rifts can even occur between individuals who have been friends for decades. I have personally experienced such situations and acknowledge that I have often contributed to them. Nevertheless, it's a painful experience as you reflect on it, causing you to wonder if, perhaps, you're similar to me. You contemplate what more you could have done, thinking about the actions you should or shouldn't have taken. This reflection forces you to confront your limitations as you navigate the loss of that relationship. Later in the book, we will delve into strategies not just for coping but for effectively managing the challenges associated with limitations and losses, especially within the context of relationships.

Ages

Consider how limitations and losses are readily evident in our developmental stages as human beings. From the moment of conception and throughout our early years, we grapple with profound dependence and significant limitations. This reality persists through the conception and birthing process. As a newborn enters the world, it remains markedly limited, requiring substantial assistance and being scarcely self-sufficient. Moreover, it is highly susceptible to various forms of loss and vulnerable to diseases and threats that may endanger, harm, or infect it. However, as this infant matures, it gradually transcends many of its limitations and outgrows numerous losses intrinsically connected to its youth.

As children develop, they progress through adolescence, gaining strength and building immunity against common ailments like colds and the flu. This growth leads to increased independence, and most parents are well acquainted with these developmental stages. However, a significant transformation occurs as individuals transition into their teenage years, continue into their twenties, and reach their thirties. During this period, humans reach the pinnacle of their strength and capabilities. If they have maintained their well-being, they are at their healthiest. Many limitations that were prominent during adolescence become obsolete and no longer restrict them.

The process of human development follows a discernible pattern. Initially, during our early years, we face significant limitations and susceptibility to loss, which is often outgrown as we progress through adolescence into our teenage years and young adulthood. This stage, spanning from our twenties to our thirties and early forties, marks a period of reduced constraints and greater independence.

However, this trend shifts as we continue to age, experiencing a return to limitations. This shift is particularly evident among the elderly population. They were the most vulnerable group during the COVID-19 pandemic, and they remain at higher risk for illnesses such as the flu due to the weakening of their immune systems with age. Therefore, as we reach our fifties, sixties, seventies, and eighties, we become increasingly exposed to limitations and losses once more.

Personally

Consider the various facets of your life as you read along, focusing on your own personal development. As individuals striving for growth, self-awareness, improved relational skills, enhanced personal abilities, and greater vocational effectiveness, we inevitably encounter limitations and losses.

This dynamic also manifests in our aspiration to lead moral and virtuous lives, both in our relationships with loved ones and our conduct within the countries we call home. We aim to exhibit justice, kindness, and love and avoid harmful and criminal behaviors. However, despite our daily intentions to be good, loving, patient, and kind individuals, we must honestly acknowledge that there are times when we fall short of our aspirations. In these moments, we find ourselves facing limitations and losses once more. At times, our own actions may directly lead to these losses.

In my own life, it's a recurring reality that many of the losses I've experienced don't solely stem from external events, circumstances, or the actions of others. Rather, they are often a direct consequence of my own actions or my lack of action.

Furthermore, we encounter limitations and losses within our capabilities. With age comes a heightened awareness of our strengths and weaknesses. Some individuals are prone to frustration due to these limitations, while others adopt a more passive approach. Nevertheless, we all confront the inescapable reality that our lives are governed by constraints: limited time, finite abilities, and a finite intellect. There are moments when life demands more from us, but we find ourselves incapable of meeting those demands. Similarly, we sometimes desire to remain present in a particular moment yet lack the emotional and physical endurance required to do so.

We encounter limitations and their consequences, often resulting in loss, in various aspects of our lives. This extends metaphorically to our personal experiences, where our limitations can lead to tangible losses. Additionally, we confront these limitations on a physical level, as I've previously discussed in the preceding chapter regarding the effects of aging. Recognizing that my readers encompass diverse stages of life, I'm aware that many of you are contending with physical limitations and experiencing physical losses. Personally, I'm now in a phase where I require reading glasses, find myself unable to perform certain movements, and have had to adapt my exercise routine due to the gradual physical changes and limitations that come with aging. This is a testament to the presence of both physical limitations and resulting losses within me.

Emotionally, we can observe changes in our emotional capacity over time, with the potential for it to expand or diminish as we age, which leads us to confront its limitations and accompanying losses. These dynamics manifest mentally and spiritually, as we've previously discussed. Furthermore, these patterns are evident in our relationships with others. Upon self-examination, we recognize that both limitations and losses are present within us, impacting various aspects of our lives in diverse ways.

Religion

In the realm of religion, several instances clearly reveal the existence of limitations and losses. A prominent example pertains to the adherents of religion. A significant deterrent to the widespread adoption of religions is the perceived hypocrisy among its followers. It is essential to distinguish between genuine hypocrisy and individuals who may struggle to adhere entirely to religious doctrines and principles. Engaging with religion, whether as a practitioner or observer, invariably exposes one to these limitations, as it's unrealistic to expect flawless adherence. While this isn't an excuse, it provides an explanatory framework for the observed human imperfections in religious practice. Hypocrisy, on the other hand, remains indefensible, especially when individuals openly and unrepentantly act in direct contradiction to their professed religious beliefs.

Devoted followers within any religion inevitably fall short of perfection, and anyone asserting otherwise should be regarded skeptically, as they may be deluding themselves. Loss is another facet of religion, as many practitioners, before gaining anything, frequently experience substantial losses. Some individuals have even sacrificed their lives in the pursuit of their religious beliefs. In religious practice, people have faced the loss of family members, spouses, children, and employment. As exemplified by the COVID-19 pandemic, certain individuals, motivated by religious convictions, refused vaccinations and suffered significant losses. Thus, limitations and losses are evident in the practice of religion.

An illustrative narrative from the 'New Testament of the Bible, specifically one of the Gospels, recounts a moment when Jesus, in the final stages of his life, sought solace in a garden to pray. During this distressing period, Jesus confronted the imminent prospect of arrest, trial, and crucifixion. He requested a couple of his disciples to accompany him, stay awake, and pray alongside him. Upon entering the garden, Jesus engaged in prayer three times. After each instance, he returned to his disciples, only to discover them asleep. One of Jesus's statements stands out, emphasizing the concept of limitations and losses. One time, when Jesus came back to them, Jesus remarked, "The spirit is willing, but the flesh is weak."

This encapsulates the idea of limitations and losses. The loss Jesus experienced was that his friends, whom he had asked to support him during this crucial and challenging period, were unable to remain awake and pray with him.

Jesus encountered the loss of their absence, but he didn't attribute it to their malice. He recognized it as a result of their limitations. The Gospel provides further context, explaining that their drowsiness occurred in the middle of the night after a long day, leading to their tiredness. Many of us can relate to this from personal experience because we've all nodded off during a movie, a conversation, or when we're simply fatigued. Falling asleep represents a limitation, while the other person perceives a loss. This illustrates the interplay of limitations and losses in religion. Additionally, within the realm of religion, we should consider our relationship with God.

While practicing religion, many individuals face an aspect that is not frequently discussed, even though it's a prevalent reality. Surprisingly, various religious texts are quite candid about this issue. It concerns the followers of a religion experiencing limitations in their relationship with God. This goes beyond their devotion or their desire to love God; it pertains to God's responses to their petitions and prayers. When these requests are not answered in the expected manner or time frame, the followers encounter a limitation within their religious practice and experience a genuine loss. These are significant realities to acknowledge.

Government

In the current global events, one cannot help but notice the multi-faceted role that governments play on the world stage. Governments are tasked with a wide array of responsibilities, and while they may excel in certain areas, they often fall short in others. This intricate interplay between government action and inaction reveals the stark reality that, despite their promises and good intentions, governments sometimes prove incapable of fulfilling their commitments.

The limitations that governments encounter are both multifarious and frequently all too evident. They may grapple with resource constraints, bureaucratic inefficiencies, or the challenges of navigating the intricacies of international relations. The consequences of these limitations can be far-reaching and impact the lives of their citizens. For instance, in times of economic hardship or crisis, governments may struggle to provide adequate support and relief to their people, leading to financial hardship and loss among their citizenry.

Furthermore, governments can inadvertently become catalysts for loss among their citizens through their policies and decisions. In our roles as citizens, we are not merely passive observers but active participants in the democratic process. We elect our leaders, entrusting them with the responsibility of making decisions that will affect our lives and our futures. However, there are times when these decisions result in practical repercussions that lead to limitations and losses in our daily lives.

For example, government decisions regarding public health and safety can directly influence our well-being. During public health crises, the government's actions, or lack thereof, can have a profound impact on the health and safety of citizens. Inadequate responses, delays in policy implementation, or the misallocation of resources can lead to loss of life and well-being.

Moreover, government actions can also contribute to economic losses. Decisions related to taxation, trade policies, or financial regulations can affect the financial stability of individuals and businesses. Additionally, government actions in areas like education and infrastructure development can influence future opportunities and quality of life for citizens.

In essence, the dynamic relationship between governments and citizens is one marked by both potential and peril. Governments, despite their limitations, hold the power to effect positive change, uphold justice, and safeguard the well-being of their people. However, when government decisions or actions fall short, the consequences can be felt in the form of limitations and losses among the citizenry. In this delicate balance, citizens play a crucial role in holding their governments accountable, advocating for change, and actively participating in the democratic process to ensure that government actions align with the needs and aspirations of the people they serve.

Politics

The realm of politics, intricately interwoven with the government but possessing its unique dynamics, provides a stark illustration of both limitations and losses. It's worth noting that many of the aspects discussed in the context of government apply to politics, but politics often offers an even more distinct example of these challenges. In this intricate arena, politicians, those entrusted with governing and making pledges concerning the government and their own actions, frequently demonstrate an inability to fulfill their commitments. This incapacity represents a significant limitation within the political landscape.

Simultaneously, politicians, in their pursuit and implementation of policies, can be direct catalysts for losses experienced by us, the citizens they represent. Whether it's through economic policies that affect livelihoods, foreign policy decisions that shape international relations, or social policies that impact civil rights and social justice, political actions have profound implications for our lives. The consequences of these actions can manifest as losses in various forms, ranging from financial hardships to limitations on individual freedoms.

Moreover, the contemporary political landscape is often characterized by a prevalence of drama, discord, disputes, and, regrettably, conflicts and wars. These ongoing struggles can have a profound impact on the collective psyche of citizens. In some instances, disillusionment with the political process has led many individuals to disengage from political discussions, education, or active participation. This disengagement stems from a perception that politics is not only ineffectual but also highly restricted in its ability to bring about meaningful change, ultimately serving as a source of loss for those who hoped for more from their political leaders and institutions.

The inherent limitations and losses within politics underscore the complexities and challenges of this field. However, it's crucial to recognize that politics is also the arena where profound change can occur, where policies and decisions can shape the trajectory of nations and societies. While limitations and losses are intrinsic to the political process, they do not negate the potential for positive change and progress. Citizens, through their active engagement and advocacy, have the power to hold politicians accountable, shape the political agenda, and push for policies that align with their values and aspirations. In this way, politics, despite its challenges, remains a crucial vehicle for addressing societal issues and advancing the common good.

Business and organizations

In the landscape of business and organizations, individuals often find themselves navigating a complex terrain marked by the presence of limitations and losses. Whether you're an entrepreneur charting your own course or an employee contributing to a larger enterprise, the journey frequently entails a continuous quest to identify and implement solutions to overcome these obstacles. It's a pursuit that unfolds with the recognition that while some limitations and losses may be surmountable, others are inherently insurmountable.

A similar dynamic is at play within organizations themselves. Countless board meetings and strategic discussions revolve around the challenges posed by limitations and the consequences of losses, whether they pertain to financial setbacks, market volatility, or operational inefficiencies. However, it's regrettable that many leadership teams involved in these discussions often lack a perspective that interprets their experiences through the framework of limitations and losses. They may instead respond impulsively, driven by fear and anxiety rather than a comprehensive understanding of the challenges they face.

I contend that adopting a perspective rooted in the acknowledgment of limitations and losses can be transformative for businesses and organizations. Such a perspective has the potential to not only reshape their understanding of the challenges they encounter but also empower them to devise more effective and sustainable solutions. When leaders and decision-makers approach limitations and losses with a structured and strategic mindset, they are better equipped to navigate adversity, respond proactively, and harness these challenges as catalysts for growth.

Moreover, recognizing limitations and losses within the business landscape is not an exercise in defeatism but a strategic approach to better equip individuals and organizations for the road ahead. It invites a nuanced exploration of the root causes of these limitations, whether they stem from market dynamics, resource constraints, or internal factors. This introspective approach can lead to the identification of opportunities for improvement, innovation, and resilience.

In essence, the realms of business and organizations serve as fertile ground for understanding the intricate interplay between limitations and losses. They provide a platform for individuals to apply their problem-solving skills, creativity, and resilience. By adopting a perspective that acknowledges the presence of limitations and losses, individuals and organizations can harness the power of adaptive and strategic thinking to navigate the challenges they face and emerge stronger, more resilient, and better equipped for the complex and ever-changing world of business.

Death

The tapestry of life encompasses a final context where limitations and losses become starkly evident, as mentioned earlier in various situations. This context revolves around the universal experience of death, a reality that all individuals must eventually confront, regardless of their background or status. It stands as an indisputable and inescapable truth. Despite our efforts and aspirations, death is a limit that draws near inexorably, casting its shadow over our mortal existence.

Many of us tend to avoid discussing death, perhaps relegating it to the periphery of our thoughts until circumstances force us to confront its harsh reality. Yet, in the context of limitations and losses, death stands out as a profoundly visible and profound example that cannot be ignored. It represents the ultimate manifestation of human limitations and the most profound of losses.

Contemplating death forces us to face the undeniable limitations of human life. Despite our advancements in science, technology, and medicine, mortality's ultimate outcome remains unchanged. It serves as a defining limit of the human experience, prompting us to reflect on the significance of our actions, the legacy we leave, and our cherished values.

Simultaneously, death is the most profound of losses, touching lives with deep grief and sorrow. The loss of a loved one resonates deeply within the human heart and soul. It's an unquantifiable loss that leaves an indelible mark on those who remain. This loss serves as a reminder of life's transient nature and the importance of cherishing our time with loved ones.

In the face of death's undeniable presence, individuals and societies have developed various coping mechanisms and ways of finding meaning. Religion and spirituality offer solace and hope, while cultural traditions provide rituals to honor the departed. The arts, literature, and philosophy have also delved into the theme of mortality, offering insights to navigate complex emotions related to loss.

In conclusion, death is the ultimate and indisputable context where the profound realities of limitations and losses converge. It reminds us of our inherent limitations as mortal beings and underscores the enduring impact of loss on the human experience. While it may be a topic that inspires contemplation and trepidation, it also invites reflection, introspection, and a deeper appreciation for the preciousness of our time on this Earth. By acknowledging and embracing the reality of death, we can find ways to live more meaningfully, love more deeply, and approach life's limitations and losses with resilience, compassion, and understanding.

$\frac{20}{200}$

**LIMITATIONS
AND
LOSSES**

$\frac{20}{100}$

$\frac{20}{70}$

**LIMITATIONS
AND
LOSSES**

$\frac{20}{50}$

$\frac{20}{40}$

**LIMITATIONS
AND
LOSSES**

$\frac{20}{30}$

$\frac{20}{25}$

1

2

3

4

5

6

7

4

Chapter 4:
MISCONCEPTIONS OF LIMITATIONS AND LOSSES

This chapter highlights the significance of dispelling misconceptions and not relying on them to address limitations and losses, as these misconceptions are not advantageous when facing such challenges. Therefore, we will now examine some common misconceptions about limitations and losses, aiming to encourage you to adopt a more critical perspective when dealing with them. The first misconception is that limitations and losses are always negative. While we often perceive them negatively, not all limitations and losses carry a negative connotation. In fact, some limitations have positive aspects. For instance, when it comes to air travel, we appreciate that airplanes have weight limits, and we wouldn't want these limits to be violated or exceeded.

The same principle applies to losses. Some things in our lives are not beneficial for us, so the removal of those things is not necessarily a negative occurrence. Certain individuals who have been part of our lives may have had adverse effects on us, and losing their presence can actually be a positive development. Our tendency to perceive limitations and losses negatively often stems from viewing them as obstacles to our desires rather than as inherent aspects of our journey toward our goals. These are two distinct perspectives on limitations and losses. However, it's a misconception to assume that they are always useless. Additionally, we sometimes regard them as worthless, akin to mosquitoes or flies.

In reality, we often fail to discern a purpose for them beyond their capacity to irritate, inflict harm, potentially cause illness and generally make certain seasons and occasions more uncomfortable. Their presence appears devoid of purpose. However, as previously noted in the first misconception, limitations and losses can impart valuable lessons and serve as catalysts for our personal growth. They are not devoid of value; they exist for a reason. These experiences can serve as teachers, offering profound insights about ourselves, others, and how to enhance our personal effectiveness across various pursuits in our lives.

Another misconception involves the belief that they should be entirely avoided. This is a misconception primarily because complete avoidance is often unattainable. When exploring the annals of history, one can readily observe that nobody has managed to evade limitations and losses. These experiences are pervasive and enduring. Embracing the misconception that they should be entirely avoided can lead to detrimental consequences. For instance, an individual holding this belief is more likely to develop an avoidance-based personality concerning these challenges, making them susceptible to seeking excessive prescriptions to cope with limitations and losses. Some common responses to this belief include outright denial of their existence, attributing them to personal weakness, or associating them with societal structures or oppressors. Chapter five, "Origins of Limitations and Losses," will delve into this further.

The majority of limitations and losses that individuals encounter are not directly attributable to their governments or prevailing policies. Many of them are deeply ingrained within the fabric of human existence and society. Should someone adopt the notion that they can completely evade these challenges, they are likely to experience social isolation, strained relationships, immense frustration, and ultimately inhabit a delusional world. And if, by some means, an individual deludes themselves into believing they can escape the inescapable realities of limitations and losses, it would be nothing short of a tragic self-deception. The fourth misconception is that these experiences are perpetually conquerable. This hardly needs mention, given our foundational premise that they are two inescapable certainties. However, one can certainly mitigate the impact of limitations and losses.

Limitations and losses can be mitigated to some extent, and occasional victories can be won in certain battles. However, it's crucial to understand that they ultimately prevail in the grander scheme, should you choose to confront them head-on. Additionally, there are limitations and losses that simply cannot be defeated. Take, for instance, death—a universal reality that no one can escape. Similarly, sickness eventually affects everyone, as does the natural process of aging. In the realm of personal development, obstacles and setbacks are inherent to the journey of increasing self-awareness, honing relational skills, developing personal aptitudes, and enhancing vocational proficiency. Thus, the focus should shift from defeating limitations and losses to learning how to coexist with them and navigate life effectively in their presence. The fifth misconception is that all limitations and losses result from conscious choices when, in fact, some of them do not.

Indeed, most limitations and losses that we encounter are ingrained in the intricate fabric of culture, society, and the environment that envelops us. For some, it might be more convenient to assign blame for limitations and losses to another individual's conscious decisions, as it appears simpler to rectify than embracing the inherent realities of our existence. However, this outlook is rooted in the sixth misconception: the notion that you should never acknowledge limitations and losses. Some motivational speakers and social media influencers have been known to link the acceptance of these limitations and losses with weakness, an exaggerated perspective that misconstrues the essence of these challenges. This perspective invariably portrays them as exclusively negative, entirely futile, and to be steadfastly avoided, all of which I fervently challenge.

Distinguishing between recognizing a limitation or loss, accepting them, and permitting them to govern your life is essential. It's accurate to assert that allowing limitations and losses to dominate every facet of your existence is unwarranted. However, the notion that you should never acknowledge them is disagreeable to me. The critical point isn't whether you accept them but whether you acknowledge and adapt to them as you navigate life. The final misconception about limitations and losses is that they are invariable of a physical or material nature. In truth, many of the limitations and losses we confront are intangible.

These limitations and losses are encountered in ways that may not be tangible, such as our mental health, emotions, and the intricate depths of our souls. To solely perceive limitations and losses as pertaining to business endeavors, organizational ventures, or the loss of relationships, marriages, or loved ones due to death is to diminish the profound impact they exert on us as individuals.

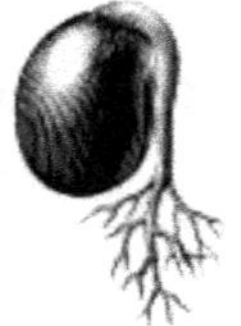

5

─────

Chapter 5: ORIGINS OF LIMITATIONS AND LOSSES

I thought it was important to include this chapter in the book for several reasons. First, the more you understand limitations and losses the better equipped you are going to be to live with them. Second, the best prescriptions are always based on the most accurate diagnosis. Knowing their genesis can help us treat them more effectively. Third, the origins of limitations and losses can comfort us as we discover that often we aren't personally responsible for their presence. Finally, it is my hope that knowing their origins will enable you to walk with those whom you love more effectively and lovingly.

The question of origins is focused on the beginning of limitations and losses. To put it simply, where did they come from? I believe they come from five places. One, creation, and when I use this term I refer to the created order. I recognize that some of my readers may not subscribe to a creation paradigm. But, my argument works with evolution or any other theory you may subscribe to because it's based on the transcendent nature of our universe, its laws and species. We find limitations and losses in every part of the observable universe. We

35

find them in laws like gravity, and of course we find them in humans and animals. There's nowhere you can look and not see limitations and losses. I believe our planet, universe and every human and animal was created with them. This is why they are so evident.

Two, they come from something Christians call the fall. The fall refers to a period of time where sin entered the world and took limitations and losses to another level. The fall answers the question: what's wrong with this world? The fall brought death into the world as we know it and also brought an immense amount of suffering, scarcity and evil. All those things bring limitations and losses with them.

Three, they come from DNA. We pass them down and sometimes they last generations. When I speak of DNA I'm talking specifically about predispositions which we inherit from our parents. Now, of course some of them can be mitigated but the fact that we have to act or think differently to do so proves how effective DNA is at transmitting limitations and losses.

Four, they come from our choices and the choices of others. We can bring them into our lives and the lives of others by the decisions we make. A good example of this is domestic abuse. These actions always bring limitations and sometimes even the loss of life. And, we now have irrefutable proof that these kinds of actions can permeate the victims of it and be transferred from one generation to another.

Five, they come from circumstances that are out of our control. There are so many scenarios that happen to us that bring limitations and losses. Parent's can't always control what their child is born with. Married couples don't have control of their spouses. Workers aren't ultimately in control of their companies budgets and whether or not they will get a raise or be fired. There are so many scenarios I could present but I think you get the point.

Types of Limitations and Losses

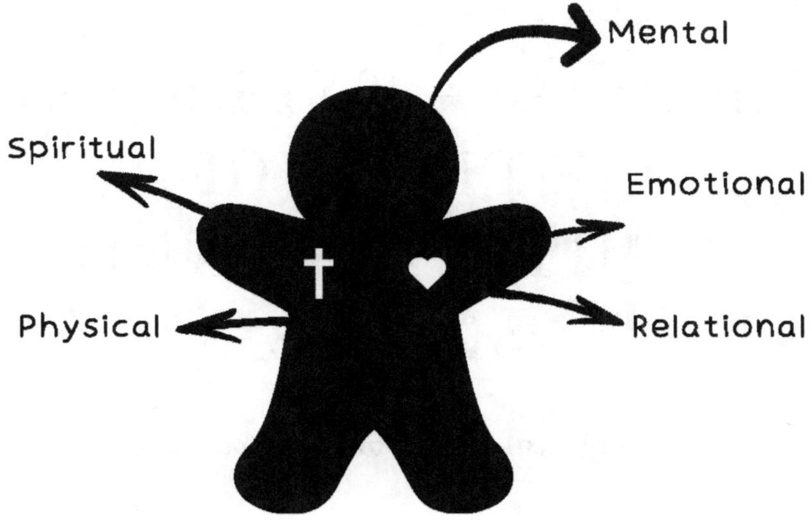

6

Chapter 6: – TYPES AND EFFECTS OF LIMITATIONS AND LOSSES

Physical limitations and losses

There are numerous physical limitations and losses that we encounter throughout our lives. Some of these limitations and losses were briefly mentioned earlier when discussing the various life stages where these limitations and losses are most apparent. When addressing our age-related development, we primarily focus on the physical limitations and losses associated with our physiological growth. The concept of physical limitations and losses is something we all acknowledge and accept, albeit often residing in our subconscious. We openly discuss these limitations and losses, adapt to them in our daily lives, and even use humor to cope with the changing dynamics as we transition between youth and old age.

Physical limitations and losses become noticeable early in life and persist as we continue to age and grow. One of the initial physical limitations or losses we encounter is the sensation of hunger or thirst, prompting our bodies to react and alter our sensations. Although we may not always perceive it as such in the moment, this is among our first experiences with physical limitations and losses. When we sustain injuries, whether it's a sprained ankle, a broken bone, or the development of a disability, we confront physical limitations and losses.

A simple injury like a sprained ankle, which usually heals completely, is still accompanied by the experience of limited movement, decreased ability, and a sense of constraint. Therefore, physical injuries commonly result in physical limitations or losses. Stress and anxiety, when encountered, affect our bodies, often leading to limitations and losses. This is manifested as reduced concentration, a depletion of stored energy reserves, and physical sensations such as an increased heart rate or a general sense of unease in the body.

The physical effects of extreme stress and anxiety have limiting and detrimental consequences. In severe cases, they can lead to absenteeism from work or necessitate downtime, resulting in various losses, including in relationships and the ability to perform tasks. These effects are undeniably limitations. Individuals born with physical disabilities also experience lasting limitations and losses. In the US, a substantial portion, estimated at over 20 percent, grapples with disabilities, most of which manifest as physical challenges. It's crucial to acknowledge their full humanity and equal worth, yet they encounter daily limitations and losses.

Some readers may have personal experience with physical limitations and losses, whether they were born with such conditions or are caregivers, friends, loved ones, or family members of individuals facing daily challenges. The disability community is acutely aware of these physical limitations and losses. In Western prosperous cultures, these limitations manifest in various ways, such as the presence of wheelchair ramps and accessible bathrooms. Importantly, it should be recognized that everyone possesses inherent physical limitations and will inevitably encounter losses due to injuries, aging, and, ultimately, death, which is the ultimate loss.

A scenario exists in which a previously healthy individual with considerable abilities might encounter a situation akin to a disability. For instance, a close friend of mine received a diagnosis of stage four kidney disease a couple of years ago. During a conversation while taking a walk, I broached the topic of limitations, losses, and disabilities, and encouraged him to perceive his stage four kidney disease as a disability. I suggested that he should operate with this outlook, embracing it as both a limitation and a loss. The objective was not to surrender completely, becoming inert and passive, but to adopt it as a life-altering perspective. I distinctly remember the contemplative expression on his face as he processed this idea.

In conclusion, concerning physical limitations and losses, these are aspects we may encounter in our daily lives. Experiencing illness, allergies, the flu, or sleep disruptions can disrupt our typical physical and physiological patterns, resulting in various degrees of limitation and loss. Many of the individuals reading this book are likely familiar with the effects of sleepless nights and how they can impact their physical well-being. Parents caring for young children may especially understand these challenges. There exist direct connections between our daily routines, encompassing rest, nutrition, and exercise, and how deviations from these routines can affect us physically, leaving enduring imprints of limitations and losses.

Mental limitations and losses

In our exploration of physical limitations and losses, we must also address their mental counterparts. It is widely acknowledged that, in alignment with the diversity of our human bodies and minds, there exists a range of mental capacities. Individuals vary in their mental aptitude, leading to differences in the extent to which they experience mental limitations and losses. Some are endowed with vast mental capacity, which minimizes the impact of such limitations and losses. Conversely, those born with mental disabilities face numerous limitations and losses due to their conditions. However, akin to physical limitations and losses, we can also encounter mental constraints and setbacks due to specific life circumstances.

Imagine your routine day proceeding smoothly, but then you receive a phone call delivering news that a cherished individual has received a terminal cancer diagnosis or been involved in a severe car accident. Instantly, the mental freedom and capacity you previously possessed are drained and consumed by the weight of that phone call. Similar to the realm of the physical, the mental domain also exposes us to daily experiences of limitations and losses. Furthermore, just as we recognize that physical abilities decline with age, we must acknowledge that there is a tipping point where our mental capacities and capabilities deteriorate, culminating in various forms of loss.

Alzheimer's dementia is a leading disease in America today and it's essentially the attack of the brain memory loss, accompanied by memory loss and, at times, hallucinations, leading to a diminished capacity to function as previously experienced. Numerous individuals have encountered this debilitating condition. For instance, I am acquainted with a young man who, prior to an accident, exhibited remarkable mental acuity. However, following the accident, his mental processing speed markedly declined. This demonstrates that external circumstances can exert a profound influence on the aspects we are discussing. Furthermore, certain phases of life are inherently more demanding than others, further accentuating these limitations and losses.

The nature of your profession significantly influences your exposure to limitations and losses. For example, if you are currently serving in the military in 2023, you may contend with a multitude of limitations and losses due to the prevailing global circumstances, such as the looming threat of war and the prospect of deployment. Occupations like law enforcement or emergency services, which demand unwavering concentration and daily exposure to peril, inherently carry a heightened risk of encountering limitations and losses. In some vocations, facing these challenges is an integral part of the job description.

Mitigating mental limitations and losses is possible through various strategies like maintaining a habit of reading and meditation, along with proper diet and exercise. Nevertheless, it's essential to acknowledge that as we age, our cognitive faculties will naturally decline, and eventually, we will lose them in death. Therefore, it is crucial to stay attuned to our life stage and season, always remaining open to opportunities for rejuvenation and necessary adjustments concerning mental limitations and losses.

Mental burnout is akin to running out of fuel if we compare our brains to a car. As a writer, this phenomenon is often referred to as writer's block. It occurs when individuals typically brimming with ideas and enthusiasm for creating fresh content suddenly encounter a creative wall and find themselves devoid of inspiration. Mental limitations and losses give rise to introspective thoughts about our capacities, sometimes leading to harsh self-judgment and self-critical internal dialogues like, "Why couldn't I come up with that?" or "What's wrong with me?" Such experiences are common when grappling with mental limitations and losses.

Emotional limitations and losses

Emotional limitations and losses are an inherent aspect of our human experience. Our emotions, like our mental and physical aspects, possess a certain capacity. This emotional capacity can be developed and expanded upon, but we are also born with a preexisting emotional disposition that is beyond our control. Some individuals are naturally inclined to have vast emotional reservoirs, akin to an expansive ocean teeming with a wide array of emotions, constituting a rich emotional ecosystem. In contrast, others may have a more limited emotional capacity, resembling a compact fish tank.

Emotionally, we exist on a spectrum with varying capacities, much like a fish tank that contains life but is distinct from an ocean. It's essential for us to cultivate self-awareness and recognize where we fall on this spectrum or if we're somewhere in between. Our evaluation of our emotional capacity, similar to how we assess our mental abilities, can be a source of emotional limitations and losses. At times, we tend to be excessively judgmental and self-critical. As emotional beings, our responses to life's experiences are inherently emotional. While some may resist this aspect of our nature, it's essential to acknowledge that we are fundamentally emotional creatures, and attempts to suppress our emotions are counterproductive. When we encounter life's challenges, our emotional responses often bring about limitations.

A concrete example illustrates how emotions can impose limitations on our actions. On December 15, 2019, at three in the afternoon, I received a phone call informing me of my mother's passing. The immediate flood of emotions I experienced hindered my ability to proceed with my scheduled celebratory dinner with staff that evening. Emotionally, I was no longer prepared or willing to attend the dinner. Instead, I had to address various matters related to my mother's passing, such as visiting her body and making necessary decisions, which evoked a wide array of emotions.

During this period, I had the challenging responsibility of informing all my brothers and sisters, which led to numerous discussions and inquiries about funeral arrangements. However, the overwhelming emotional turmoil I was experiencing made it impossible for me to contemplate such practical matters. My primary focus was on coping with the profound loss of my mother, which was being exacerbated by the intense emotions I was grappling with. Emotions, which manifest as responses to the stimuli we encounter in life through our senses and experiences, frequently introduce limitations and losses into our lives. One prevalent and potent emotion in today's culture is depression.

At this juncture, it's important to acknowledge that while depression does involve psychological elements, it is not limited to mere thoughts. It is a deeply felt emotional experience. When individuals grapple with severe depression, it is not only a matter of thinking about it; they also feel the weight of it. Acute depression stands as a significant contributor to the emergence of limitations and losses in one's life. In terms of loss, the most tragic outcome of depression is when it progresses to the point where suicidal thoughts start to take hold, leading individuals to choose to end their own lives rather than endure the agony of prolonged depression. This decision represents a profound loss. However, for those who opt not to take such a drastic step, they must contend with substantial limitations. Some individuals may find themselves retreating into isolation, seeking solace in specific forms of music, or relying on medication and therapy to manage their condition.

In certain cases, emotions can operate as a type of disability, specifically an emotional one, hindering individuals from functioning in their usual capacity, both in their professional and personal lives. Emotions, including pain, can impose limitations and result in losses for all of us. Addressing our emotional wounds, which often underlie our pain, is a key aspect of managing these effects. Pain itself is inherently limiting and typically leads to losses, with these effects becoming most apparent in our relationships, professional endeavors, and overall abilities. To summarize, emotions can serve as driving forces, enhancing our capabilities and propelling us forward, but they can also bring about limitations and losses. In navigating this complex landscape, self-awareness and personalized treatment strategies play crucial roles in our pursuit of a well-rounded and fulfilling life.

Spiritual limitations and losses

This topic is included in the book because I recognize that, personally, I often do not give it the attention it deserves, and I believe it's essential to do so. Typically, when we contemplate spirituality, it's as if we are seeking a solution that transcends our human nature. Many of us turn to spirituality to counteract the constraints of our humanity, our physical limitations, and the limitations of our flesh. We perceive spirituality as a kind of superpower that swoops in to enable us to achieve remarkable feats. While there's some validity to this perspective, it can sometimes be taken to an extreme, and that's what I aim to discuss here. To clarify further, at times, we regard religion and spirituality as the remedy for our physical and relational limitations and losses, acknowledging the truths within this viewpoint.

However, it's crucial to recognize that our spirituality also carries its own set of limitations and losses, and this is what I intend to explore. To illustrate this, I'd like to revisit an example I mentioned earlier in this book, one that is familiar to many people around the world. As previously discussed, there's an incident in the book where Jesus was in a garden with his friends just before his impending death. He had requested that they stay awake with him, but they repeatedly fell asleep. Upon returning to them after his prayers, he made a significant statement, "The spirit is willing, but the flesh is weak." We've delved into the meaning of this statement earlier.

What I would like to emphasize from that statement is the inter-connectedness of our spirit and our physical being. Our spirituality is not entirely independent from our physicality; they coexist and are co-dependent. This means that our spirituality is, in a sense, housed within our physicality, and as we've previously explored, our physicality has its own set of limitations and losses. Consequently, our spirituality must also possess limitations and experience losses. Just like our physical, mental, and emotional aspects, our spirits require development and are not inherently unchanging. In religious terms, our spirits may undergo regeneration and rebirth, but they, too, have room for growth and are susceptible to limitations, losses, and failures.

Let's consider this spiritual aspect. Many of us are seekers, constantly trying to establish a connection with the divine. This connection is often pursued through prayer, meditation, or the study of sacred texts and our responses to them. However, we frequently encounter limi-tations throughout this process, whether they arise from sleepiness, fatigue, anxiety, or preoccupations. Additionally, inherent weaknesses exist within our spirits and our spirituality. It's important to under-stand that our spirituality cannot conquer every obstacle in life. While some may present a different perspective, I respectfully disagree. In simple terms, countless individuals throughout human history have offered spiritual prayers that have remained unanswered.

When a prayer is offered, whether it's for a family member, a friend, or even oneself, and it goes unanswered, it leads to a sense of limitation and loss. Many individuals grapple with the perplexing situation because, as previously noted, spirituality is often perceived as the heroic savior, and we are at a loss when our hero falters or appears incapable of rescuing us. Such moments challenge us profoundly, and some may respond by entirely abandoning their spiritual or religious beliefs. They question the extent to which spirituality can truly offer help, expressing sentiments like, "I prayed, but it didn't save my grandmother," "I prayed, but it couldn't protect my children," or "I prayed, and yet I found myself in these miserable circumstances."

This serves as a prominent illustration of the daily spiritual limitations and losses that necessitate our consideration. These experiences can lead to feelings of despair and disconnection from spirituality. In contemporary times, a prevalent response is deconstruction, reflecting our struggle with why spirituality appears to fall short. Questions abound, questioning the authenticity of religious practices, the presence of hypocrisy within religious circles, and even self-reflection on personal integrity. The evident spiritual limitations and losses become more pronounced when we take a closer examination. There's one more significant effect to mention—when we encounter spiritual limitations and losses, we frequently permit them to influence our faith and spiritual journey.

When confronted with spiritual limitations and losses, they often become the primary influences shaping our perceptions of God. In other words, our diverse beliefs about God are frequently rooted in these spiritual limitations and losses. If you show me someone with certain beliefs and a creed about God, I can guarantee that their spiritual limitations and losses play a pivotal role in those convictions. For instance, individuals who acknowledge their spiritual limitations and losses often seek a God who can offer salvation, assistance, and support when they are unable to help themselves. Conversely, some people, when faced with limitations and losses, witness their concept of God diminishing in significance. This, in turn, may lead them down the path toward agnosticism and even atheism.

Relational limitations and losses

When discussing relational limitations and losses, we are primarily addressing our relationships with one another. This encompasses our relationships with our parents, siblings, extended family, and friends, whether they exist within the contexts of church, work, community, neighborhoods, or the global connections we establish through technology. This concept should be evident to all readers, as everyone has experienced a failed attempt to love someone at some point in their lives. I'm not here to determine who was right or wrong in such situations; what's clear is that these failed connections represent instances of limitations and losses.

Within the human experience, relationships stand out as one of the most evident domains where limitations and losses become apparent. We each personally aspire to enrich our relationships with health, love, positivity, and encouragement. However, our own physical, mental, emotional, and spiritual limitations and losses often hinder our ability to contribute as we desire. Paradoxically, our contributions to a relationship can occasionally trigger limitations and losses. This is an enduring, universally experienced aspect of human history which none of us can avoid. Inevitably, you will encounter relational limitations and losses, particularly due to your own limitations. Additionally, various circumstances and reasons lead to relationship failures, causing us to lose connections that were once integral to our lives.

Much like the other experiences we've discussed, the abundance of pain within relationships can lead us to become avoidant in our relational pursuits. Alternatively, we might adopt a superficial approach to relationships or approach them in a utilitarian manner, seeking only what is expedient, driven by our desire to evade the pervasive feelings of limitations and losses. These strategies aim to mitigate the impact of these experiences, but we are aware that they only offer limited relief. The effects of these limitations and losses within relationships manifest physically, potentially causing sickness, despondency, or anxiety. On a mental level, our thoughts may take a darker, angrier turn, possibly leading to depression. Emotionally, we encounter the full spectrum of feelings within relationships.

We've previously delved into how all these factors significantly contribute to the emergence of limitations and losses in our lives. It's essential for us to acknowledge that we do indeed have a part to play within our relationships, yet our role isn't all-encompassing or ultimate. Instead, our role is fundamentally contributory. Successful relationships require the active involvement of two or more individuals who interact in a healthy, humble, and persistent manner. In the absence of these qualities, we will inevitably encounter limitations and losses for which there may be no straightforward remedy.

SPECIAL MESSAGE FOR RELATIONAL LIMITATIONS AND LOSSES

I want to address those individuals who are currently grappling with relational limitations and losses. The reason I wish to discuss this matter at this juncture is because I, too, am facing these challenges alongside you. This experience can be exceedingly painful and isolating. If we were to examine it from a sociological perspective, it is likely the primary driver of personal dysfunction, self-harm, despair, and a general sense of unhappiness. In essence, it might be the foremost source of human misery. I'd like to take a moment to acknowledge, contemplate, and openly discuss this, allowing it the recognition and attention it deserves. My intention is to speak directly to a specific group of individuals at this point.

Leaders

First, I would like to speak to leaders. Leadership has been a topic of extensive discussion and coverage across various media, and I won't reiterate all of that. What I want to emphasize is the extreme importance of relationality in leadership. When I say "everything is relational," I mean precisely that. It's possible that there are leaders reading this who are currently enduring challenging times. Our companies, organizations, and households might be grappling with difficulties, but I believe that encountering relational limitations and losses is one of the most daunting challenges one can face. So, leader, you may have encountered this sentiment previously, but I want to reiterate that you are not alone. The day you embraced a leadership role, you essentially accepted the responsibility of contending with significant relational obstacles, as leading people is a complex endeavor, particularly in terms of aligning everyone's objectives.

In leadership, it remains challenging to guide and manage individuals, even when everyone shares the same goals. The intricate task of assisting people as they navigate their personal limitations and losses as they confront their unique circumstances is demanding. At times, leaders may find themselves caught in the turmoil, personally experiencing a multitude of limitations and losses. To all leaders, I extend a reassuring message: You will persevere. You will emerge from this experience intact, having gained valuable insights and grown as a leader. It's important to recognize that the two most influential factors that mold a leader are financial losses and fractured relationships, despite our wish that this were not the case.

Nevertheless, take heart, for even in the midst of these losses, you are never left empty-handed. They offer you valuable lessons to foster growth and enhance your leadership capabilities. It is your duty to accept these lessons with courage and integrate them into your future leadership endeavors.

Parents

This message is also directed towards parents, as I, too, am a parent to five children who are currently at various stages of life. I understand the illusion that parents are in control, only to realize later that such control is elusive, and in reality, we are far from having it. I am well-acquainted with the desire to provide the best for one's child, yet having to witness them make their own choices, whether they lead to positive outcomes or adversity. As a parent, I've experienced feelings of limitations and losses.

I've shed tears, sought therapy, experienced depression, and grappled with anger due to these challenges. My parenting journey has been marked by both missteps and wise decisions as a result of these limitations and losses. I've navigated a wide spectrum of emotions and experiences in the realm of parenting. I want to assure you that you're not alone, abnormal, or at fault. You're entirely normal. If you've reached a point where you feel lost, unsure of your next move, welcome to the club. There are seasons of misery, but there are also moments of sheer joy. Just like I would advise a leader, I encourage you to take that next step, draw your next breath, and embark on your next course of action.

Embrace the wisdom that limitations and losses offer and use it as an opportunity for growth, striving to become an even better parent. It's essential to acknowledge that once your children reach the age of twelve, thirteen, or fourteen, they are essentially young adults. While you're technically still the authority figure, you're no longer entirely in control because they have a degree of autonomy. Teenagers can make their own choices, even if it means leaving the house at two in the morning. Some readers might relate to this scenario, "That's exactly what my kid did!" and you're in mourning, and you're grieving because you can't find your kid anymore.

Parenting comes with its share of painful limitations and losses, yet these experiences have the potential to shape and enrich your character.

To harness these lessons, it's essential to embrace humility, learn from your challenges, foster personal growth, and approach your role with intentionality. Additionally, find the strength to let go, make peace with your past actions, and acknowledge your imperfections. Extend apologies for any mistakes, pain, or misjudgments you've caused. Then, express your sincere desire for forgiveness and declare your commitment to moving forward with the hope of restoring, reconciling, healing, and pursuing overall well-being. At some point, as parents, we have to realize our kids grow up and become human beings, and they have to go through the cycle. And we need to move from being coaches, quote unquote owners, to fans who put our kids' jerseys on. Go sit in the stands, grab the popcorn and the Coke, and watch our kids. And when they do a bad play, we mourn. And when they do a good play, we cheer. And at the end of the day, we never change jerseys because we're loyal to our kids.

Married people, boyfriends, girlfriends, partners.

Sociologically, it remains a fact that the parent-child relationship is one of the most challenging and painful connections in existence. However, if it's not the most challenging, then another candidate would likely be some form of partnership, whether you're involved with a boyfriend, girlfriend, or married. When engaged in these relationships, you are inevitably bound to encounter, as you are acutely aware, various forms of limitations and losses.

What I want to emphasize once more is that you are not alone. Your experiences are entirely normal, and you possess the capacity to grow through them. Indeed, there are moments when it's tremendously challenging, but there's also room for growth. Some of you have endured profound losses, and you might currently find yourself in a stage similar to my own, feeling somewhat adrift. It's natural to be unsure of what to do, especially when a significant relationship that has been a cornerstone of your life has vanished. The reasons for its disappearance may vary – perhaps due to your actions, theirs, or a combination of both, where the limitations and losses within the relationship added up to a loss. But remember, you are not alone in this experience; there are countless individuals around the world who have gone through the same things.

It's crucial to remember that you are not the worst person in the world, even if you played a role in the relationship's outcome. You're not the worst person in the world simply for experiencing it. What I'm emphasizing is that these are genuine consequences of limitations and losses in relationships. They may not always be pleasant, but, as I've mentioned earlier, they invariably offer us valuable lessons. There's something transformative in the pain and discomfort, something that can shape our souls if we permit it to do so. While this is indeed a serious aspect of the book, I hope it also serves as a source of encouragement. I hope that, like me, you are committed to taking the next breath and the next step forward.

RECIPE
Prebirth Circumstances
Family of origin
Life Circumstances
Physical factors
Personal choices

Chapter 7: FIVE COMMON CAUSES OF LIMITATIONS AND LOSSES

Pre-birth circumstances refer to the conditions and events that occurred before your birth, which had a significant impact on your birth itself and your inherent predispositions. To illustrate this, consider my mother's experience. She was born in 1931 in the southern part of the US, during a period marked by the presence of Jim Crow racism, which significantly influenced her. In contrast, I was born in 1968, a year historically known for a significant civil rights movement and racial unrest in the US Notably, Martin Luther King was assassinated on April 4, 1968, and I was born on February 6 of the same year.

The context of your birth plays a crucial role in shaping your identity and subsequently influences how you experience and process limitations and losses. It's essential to clarify that these insights are not meant to serve as excuses but rather as explanations. The primary goal of this book is to raise awareness about the nature, origins, and management of limitations and losses. Pre-birth circumstances existed and they contributed to the formation and character of your parents, who, in turn, raised you. These pre-birth circumstances left a mark on them, which consequently left a mark on you. It's imperative to acknowledge these factors. You might wonder how to go about this. If your parents are still alive, a constructive step is to engage in open conversations and ask them questions.

If your parents are no longer available, you can approach their siblings. If that option is unavailable as well, consult individuals from their generation. Ask them inquisitive questions such as "What was happening in 1968?" or "What were the circumstances in September 2001?" Gain insights into the culture, parental concerns, the educational system, and the prevailing sociological morals of the time because these aspects undeniably had an impact on how your parents nurtured you, influenced you, and imparted their teachings. Understanding your pre-birth circumstances can provide valuable insights into your approach to limitations and losses and the reasons behind their presence in your life.

Your family of origin, a topic closely linked with your pre-birth circumstances, holds distinctive significance as it concerns the individuals directly responsible for your upbringing. Whether you were raised in a two-parent household, a single-parent household, or through adoption, the critical point is comprehending the dynamics, values, concerns, and beliefs of those who raised you. It is vital to recognize that these elements become deeply ingrained within us, shaping our perceptions and how we process the world around us. This perspective and processing significantly influence how we navigate the challenges of limitations and losses, including whether we contribute to them ourselves and how we respond to them. The concept of family origin's importance becomes particularly intriguing when discussed, especially in religious settings.

Certain individuals, particularly within religious audiences, have occasionally regarded my discussions on this topic with a degree of skepticism, implying that it delves into psychological jargon. Nevertheless, it's worth noting that when examining the major religions globally, it's difficult to find any that aren't profoundly influenced by stories related to family origins. In essence, the sacred texts of these religions predominantly revolve around the experiences of people and their families, encompassing their errors, triumphs, and faith. It strikes me as ironic that this isn't a more prominent subject in our pursuit of self-awareness, especially when we seek to comprehend the individual limitations and losses we encounter. There exists a strong possibility that the limitations and losses you face personally are the same ones your family of origin confronted. Therefore, grasping the dynamics of your family of origin is foundational.

Your personal circumstances are critical. This refers to things such as your birthplace. Was it in a freezing or hot climate? Did you come from a wealthy or impoverished neighborhood? Were you raised in a blue-collar, white-collar, or working-class family? What was the social climate like? Were you constantly on the move, or did you have a steady routine? Was there any abuse in your life? Your early relationships are a primary focus here. Were they functioning or dysfunctional, beneficial or harmful, abusive or beneficent? Understanding these life conditions allows us to go deeper into the root causes of our restrictions and losses. It's worth mentioning that the insights I'm providing have a wide range of applications when we attempt to obtain a better understanding of ourselves in the arena of relationships.

Lastly, personal choices play a significant role in serving as root causes of limitations and losses. Consider this question: How do personal choices contribute to limitations and losses? I alluded to this concept earlier in the book. Suppose, like I did, you choose a career path such as becoming a pastor, a lawyer, an emergency room surgeon, or a first responder. In doing so, you consciously opt for a vocation that inherently confronts daily limitations and losses. These professions are fundamentally associated with such challenges—situations where you can't save everyone, where you can't assist everyone, and where you help some individuals who may not express gratitude. Conversely, there are those you help who are genuinely appreciative. These scenarios are the stark realities.

While government interventions and societal movements might occasionally alleviate these consequences, we must acknowledge that we will never escape the inherent limitations and losses stemming from the personal choices we make in this lifetime. Throughout my own life, I've made choices that have brought both enduring limitations and losses. Some were positive, such as becoming a parent, while others were regrettable. Due to my poor decisions, I've lost connections with some incredibly brilliant, kind, and affectionate individuals, which has resulted in limitations and losses that will persist. Yet, I am actively taking responsibility for these outcomes. These five root causes constitute the foundation of an individual's limitations and losses.

How can a better understanding of these causes lead to more effective prevention and mitigation strategies?

First, it's important to recognize that you cannot change what you're unaware of. Consequently, comprehending these five root causes of limitations and losses is the initial step in developing an effective treatment or mitigation plan. It is only after you've gained awareness of these factors that you can begin to address them.

Secondly, I firmly believe that you can't undertake this endeavor on your own, especially when it comes to creating successful prevention and mitigation strategies. You need the support of close friends, partners, loved ones, a community, or your church. There will be days when you feel overwhelmed and defeated, and that's when you'll require someone to uplift and encourage you.

I vividly recall listening to David Goggins discussing the concept of a genuine friend. According to him, a true friend is the one who, if necessary, will visit your home, knock on your door, and take you to the gym or the library, ensuring you reach your destination. In essence, a genuine friend won't allow you to fail, and we all require such friendships. When we strive to establish effective prevention and mitigation strategies in our lives, we depend on assistance.

The third point to consider is setting reasonable expectations. It's essential to remember that the objective is not to completely eliminate limitations and losses, as this is an impossible task. Instead, the aim is to discover how to coexist with them in a more efficient, comprehensive, and healthy manner.

When a neighbor experiences a limitation, such as a lack of food or the loss of a loved one, and I am aware of their challenges, my presence can be profoundly impactful. Approaching them with humility, attentiveness, and patience, I can offer support to help them move forward, guiding them through the steps needed to navigate their own limitations and losses. I believe it's important for all of us to be genuine friends and assist each other as we progress through various stages of limitations and losses.

8

Chapter 8: EMOTIONS AND THOUGHTS ASSOCIATED WITH LIMITATIONS AND LOSSES

In the domain of limitations and losses, individuals universally grapple with these challenges, each devising their unique methods to navigate them. It's crucial to recognize that limitations and losses are two inescapable facets of human existence, transcending time and affecting everyone. As we've explored in this book, their profound impact necessitates engagement and adaptation from each individual. Consequently, individuals from various parts of the world and throughout the course of history have encountered Limitations and Losses. Therefore, we can discern a common thread running through humanity, where individuals have sought ways to address these challenges, both in the past and the present. This shared human experience offers encouragement by enabling us to examine past endeavors, assessing their efficacy, and gleaning insights from contemporary strategies employed by individuals worldwide.

This book won't aim to provide an exhaustive list of psychological responses to limitations and losses, but from my extensive twenty years of experience, I've observed several prevalent psychological reactions. The foremost response is analysis. When confronted with limitations and losses, individuals often embark on a process of dissecting what these challenges entail, how they impact their lives, the specific areas where they experience their effects, the available resources to counter them, and the broader implications. Typically, the individual navigating limitations and losses engages in a mental analysis. It's important to note that much of this analytical process occurs at the subconscious level, and, truthfully, some people possess a predisposition for deeper introspection than others.

People tend to navigate life through different cognitive approaches: some are more inclined to engage in intellectual analysis, while others rely on their emotions or instincts. Nevertheless, when it comes to limitations and losses, all individuals engage in some form of assessment and analysis. As mentioned earlier, you'll discover this aspect of analysis in every person to some degree. It's the first prevalent psychological response.

The second psychological response is *hopelessness.* While there was some consideration of categorizing it as an emotion, hopelessness is essentially a thought that, when entertained, subsequently triggers a corresponding feeling. It is characterized by the perception that resources have been depleted, there is no apparent way out, and no external rescue is forthcoming. Furthermore, it encompasses the belief that there is no way to navigate the situation. These thoughts and perceptions are common psychological responses to limitations and losses. It's important to recognize that the severity of hopelessness varies, reflecting the range of limitations and losses people experience. It spans from a mild sense of hopelessness to an extreme form where an individual becomes entirely pessimistic, harboring no optimism regarding potential outcomes when facing limitations and losses.

Another psychological response to limitations and losses is the perception of *inadequacy*. When individuals grapple with these challenges, it often triggers feelings of personal inadequacy. Those facing limitations and losses frequently confront thoughts that suggest they are somehow insufficient. This sense of inadequacy emerges from their attempts to combat, overcome, or address these limitations and losses and the belief that their efforts aren't yielding the desired results. Similar to hopelessness, the spectrum of inadequacy varies from mild to severe. People experiencing a high degree of inadequacy often require substantial encouragement because dealing with limitations and losses can deplete their resources and test their character. Parents of children or caregivers for loved ones with disabilities, those living with permanent physical or mental limitations, individuals impacted by war, or those who have experienced tragic loss all grapple with this psychological response. In the face of these limitations and losses, they may perceive themselves as failing, leading to self-doubt and self-criticism regarding their capabilities and performance.

Another psychological response to limitations and losses is the act of asking questions. *Questions* are considered one of the most potent tools at our disposal. They have the potential to drive personal growth, foster improvement in our families, organizations, businesses, and churches. When individuals confront limitations and losses, they tend to become more inquisitive. It's important to note that some people attempt to downplay these limitations and losses, as we discussed previously. However, when this is not the case, individuals frequently resort to asking questions. I mentioned earlier that one way to deal with limitations and losses is to minimize their significance, which we'll categorize as a psychological response. Yet, when people are not taking that approach, they often resort to asking questions. Even when grappling with feelings of inadequacy, individuals tend to engage in self-questioning, pondering inquiries such as "Why can't I do this?" or "Why am I not stronger?"

These questions naturally surface when confronted with limitations and losses. For instance, in the context of personal relationships, if a partnership ends, it is typical for individuals to pose questions as they encounter limitations (the partnership has dissolved) and losses (the breakup). They may wonder "What went wrong?" or "Why did he or she make that choice?" or "What could I have done differently?" Therefore, a surge in questioning often signifies the presence of limitations and losses, reflecting a natural response to these challenges.

The fifth psychological response is forming **assumptions**. When individuals confront limitations and losses, part of their psychological reaction involves an attempt to rationalize and make sense of these experiences, especially when they appear incomprehensible. There is a need to comprehend why these limitations and losses have entered one's life at a particular juncture. In many cases, making assumptions is a strategy employed to facilitate this process. Assumptions are particularly prevalent in the realm of relationships. When individuals are engaged in a relationship and are simultaneously facing a limitation and a loss, they often resort to assumptions as a coping mechanism. For instance, if someone experiences harm or harshness within a relationship, it's simpler to assume that the other person despises them, doesn't like them, or doesn't love them. This mental process is favored because it provides an explanation for the observed behavior.

Conversely, acknowledging that a person can love or like you imperfectly is more challenging, as it implies the presence of a permanent limitation. It may also cast doubt on the notion of achieving an idealized, Disney-like partnership, as it reveals that imperfection permeates even the best efforts. Thus, individuals are naturally inclined to gravitate toward assumptions as a means of making the situation more palatable. This psychological response, the tendency to form assumptions, is frequently observed in various contexts, including organizations and churches. Leaders, in particular, often resort to making assumptions when they encounter limitations and losses that impede their leadership roles. These assumptions may involve labeling individuals as evil, disliking the leader, or behaving rudely, as these explanations offer a convenient way to account for the limitations and losses they face.

Another psychological response, which can be categorized as number six, involves the racking of the brain. When individuals confront limitations and losses, they often find themselves trapped in a repetitive cycle, akin to being caught in a never-ending washing machine. They continually grapple with the same questions, emotions, and perceptions, and at times, it feels inescapable. This cycle may persist from one day to the next. It's there on Monday, lingers into Tuesday, accompanies conversations over Wednesday lunches, and even infiltrates the most significant aspects of life. Limitations and losses possess a remarkable capacity to shadow individuals and infiltrate every facet of their existence. Whether they're in bed with their spouse, partner, or children or engaged in important work-related endeavors, these limitations and losses persistently occupy their thoughts. The mind becomes consumed with ceaseless contemplation, dwelling on questions, making assumptions, experiencing feelings of hopelessness, and dwelling on inadequacies. The result is a perpetually busy mind when limitations and losses are present, often leading to exhaustion. The emotional ramifications of this will be discussed later when we delve into emotional responses to limitations and losses.

The seventh psychological response to limitations and losses is *denial*. As mentioned earlier in this book, denial is a normal and natural reaction to these challenges. It's essential to clarify that limitations and losses are two inescapable realities of human existence. Nobody has ever evaded them, and it's highly unlikely that anyone ever will. However, many people have discovered ways to coexist with these challenges and lead extraordinary lives. The concept presented in this book does not suggest that we're condemned to a perpetual state of defeat. Denial can manifest in a couple of ways psychologically. Some individuals outright refuse to acknowledge the existence of limitations and losses. They may dismiss these challenges as mere facets of life that one must overcome without excuses or complaints. While there is truth in the idea of facing life's difficulties head-on, it's essential to recognize that the denial of something is often an implicit acknowledgment of its existence. Some people employ denial as a motivational tool to propel them through limitations and losses. It's not the purpose of this book to dissuade individuals from using this strategy. If it works for you, that's valid. However, this approach may not be effective for most people. For many, gaining an understanding of what they're facing, their own inner workings, and developing tailored strategies to navigate limitations and losses is crucial. Exceptional individuals who can power through these challenges in extraordinary ways exist, and they serve as a source of inspiration. Still, it's essential to remember that everyone is different, and what works for them may not work for the majority. Denial often emerges as a psychological response to limitations and losses, but it's not a one-size-fits-all strategy.

The eighth psychological response to limitations and losses is ***exaggeration***. To clarify, this means that while it's acknowledged that limitations and losses exist, some individuals tend to magnify these challenges, perceiving them as more significant than they actually are. Throughout human history, there have been fluctuations between exaggeration and minimization of various issues and experiences.

In contemporary times, there is a noticeable inclination to exaggerate the significance of issues and experiences, which can lead to heightened sensitivity. When everything is labeled as a trauma, only a few things genuinely qualify as such. When everything is deemed anxiety-inducing, only a select few actually provoke anxiety. When everything is proclaimed as important, the true significance of events diminishes.

Exaggerating the scale of limitations and losses is a psychological response that varies from person to person and is influenced by their unique perspective. Having individuals who care about you and are honest with you can help provide a more objective view. They can offer insights into whether the perceived limitation or loss is genuinely exaggerated. However, it's important to recognize that exaggeration is a common psychological response to limitations and losses.

The ninth psychological response to limitations and losses is ***diminishment***. Unlike denial, which involves thinking that these challenges don't exist, diminishment acknowledges their presence. It's the act of recognizing limitations and losses but downplaying their impact. For instance, it's when someone is at the funeral of their child and claims to be alright, although in most cases, they likely are not. Similarly, individuals who have experienced violent assaults, live with physical disabilities, or care for loved ones facing significant challenges may engage in this response. They do so to cope with the overwhelming nature of the limitation or loss by making it seem less daunting. To ascertain whether you are diminishing a limitation or loss, seeking input from those who love and care about you and allowing them to speak honestly can be beneficial. They can provide an objective perspective. Additionally, observing how your body responds to this psychological response can offer insights. If you're engaging in excessive diminishment, it may manifest physically, leading to neglect in areas that require attention.

The tenth psychological response to limitations and losses involves *comparisons*. When individuals confront these challenges, it's common to resort to comparing themselves to others. For instance, if someone is grappling with parenting limitations, struggling to connect with or influence their child, they may naturally look at other families for reference. This could include comparing their family to the one across the street, those in their church, acquaintances on social media, or their siblings' families.

Comparing oneself to others isn't inherently wrong, as there can be valuable lessons to learn from such observations. However, this tendency to compare often emerges as a natural psychological response when facing limitations and losses. It signifies that you've encountered these challenges, prompting you to look outward and wonder how others have dealt with similar situations. Questions like "How did they cope with their mother's death?" or "How did that leader handle people turning their back on them?" are typical comparisons that arise when grappling with limitations and losses.

The final psychological response is *pessimism*, often triggered by limitations and losses. Pessimism involves the belief that everything is falling apart, that life is overwhelmingly grim, and that a bleak and desolate future awaits. The narrative revolves around the idea that there is little to be hopeful or optimistic about and that encouragement is scarce. Many readers have likely encountered individuals who embody this pessimistic outlook and wondered how they reached such a negative state. They may question why these individuals are so irritable, angry, frustrated, and difficult to relate to. The root of their pessimism may lie in living with limitations and losses. As they navigate these challenges, they experience the various psychological responses we've discussed. Their ultimate conclusion becomes a sense of detachment from life, where they perceive the world, themselves, and others as inherently negative. Their response to limitations and losses is to adopt a worldview that everything is unpleasant, they are Inadequate, and so is everyone else. Consequently, they become disengaged and adopt an attitude of indifference.

In the context of understanding psychological responses to limitations and losses, it's important to consider the corresponding emotions that accompany these experiences. The first emotion we encounter is *frustration,* which is a natural response to extended periods of limitations and losses. As discussed earlier in this book, we explored the psychological responses, including pessimism, and it's worth noting that frustration serves as fertile ground for pessimism to take root. Therefore, when individuals find themselves in prolonged states of limitations and losses, frustration often becomes a prevalent emotion. It's not uncommon for leaders, for instance, to approach me with a sense of frustration, and I can readily discern that they are contending with limitations and losses. In response, I might inquire about the specific limitations they are currently facing or the losses they have endured.

This question holds significant value for organizational leaders when individuals approach them with frustration. It's equally pertinent for parents when their children express intense frustration. Depending on the audience's comprehension of the concept of limitations and losses, you may need to rephrase the question. However, given your familiarity with this book, you can provide an explanation. You might frame it like this: "What challenges did you encounter today that left you feeling unable to cope or without a solution? What losses did you experience today, be it a friendship, a contract, or the sense of losing a relationship?" Frustration is often the initial emotional response to encountering a limitation and a loss. When limitations and losses enter the picture, they deplete our reserves, leaving us with a sense of frustration because we cannot readily overcome these challenges.

The second emotional response commonly observed is **doubt.** In these moments, doubt arises, and our prior competence and confidence can waver. What used to be clear and certain can become shrouded in uncertainty once we face a limitation or loss. Suddenly, we find ourselves questioning our actions, our purpose, and our choices. We wonder if all our past efforts were worthwhile. Doubt may lead us to question our existence, our vocation, and our past decisions, contemplating alternative paths or choices. During periods of limitations and losses, experiencing a significant amount of doubt is a normal response.

The third emotional response to limitations and losses is **anger.** Anger signifies a point at which an individual feels they've had enough and is no longer willing to remain in that situation without reacting emotionally. While they may not take physical or mental action just yet, their emotional response is to be angry. People experiencing anger when facing limitations and losses often feel this way because they don't see a way out of their predicament. They might direct their anger towards others, like the government, a religion, or even themselves, believing that someone or something is to blame for their situation. This anger is a common and natural response when confronted with limitations and losses.

Anxiety represents the fourth emotional response, manifesting as that unsettling feeling of standing on uncertain ground. It's the sensation that you don't know what lies ahead, but your instincts suggest it won't be something favorable. Anxiety involves scrutinizing your current situation, doubting its authenticity, and growing increasingly convinced that there's an unseen threat on the horizon. When dealing with limitations and losses, emotional responses often include anxiety because these limitations may be known yet unknown, as is the case with sudden deaths, which are losses followed by limitations. The immediate impact is the grief and sorrow of losing someone, but then there's the uncertainty about what comes next, leading to anxiety.

Six emotional responses to limitations and losses exist, with *grief* being one of them. In the US, cultural attention towards grief has been limited. American culture is not particularly oriented toward grieving effectively. It can be argued that to engage with grief in a culturally sensitive manner, one must seek other societies where the expression of one's inner emotions is more socially acceptable. The absence of such expression is evident in American culture, but it is more conspicuous elsewhere.

When discussing grief, we refer to a profound sorrow, misery, sadness, and anguish. Grief pertains to the emotional reaction triggered by an irreplaceable loss. It endures, lacking quick remedies. Permanent limitations lead to grief since they signify an enduring loss. Examples include the inability to walk again, the constant fear of a daughter's cancer recurrence, or the diagnosis of Alzheimer's dementia in a parent. These limitations, which culminate in eventual loss, elicit grief. Acknowledging that a long-term process has commenced where one will inevitably lose a loved one due to Alzheimer's dementia, both physically and mentally, emphasizes the reality of grief. Clearly, grief is most evident when grappling with losses, particularly in the case of death.

Sadness represents the seventh emotional response to limitations and losses. Perpetual states of sadness often indicate that individuals are grappling with these limitations and losses. In such situations, it's essential to practice active listening and empathetic communication. We should engage with our loved ones to understand the root causes of their sadness and explore potential ways to alleviate it. While we may not be able to eliminate their sources of sadness, our efforts to provide support and relief can contribute to making the world a better place.

The eighth emotional response is *exhaustion*, and it serves as a primary indicator of severe limitations or losses. Exhaustion arises when all options, be they physical, emotional, spiritual, or mental, are depleted. It signifies reaching a point of utter depletion, uncertainty, and physical distress, akin to being on the brink of finishing a race with trembling, feeling unwell, and unsure of reaching the finish line. Exhaustion often characterizes our responses during periods marked by limitations and losses. If you currently experience exhaustion, live with someone who is exhausted, or work in an environment where everyone is exhausted, it is highly probable that you are contending with limitations and losses.

While certain instances, such as the exhaustion brought on by the arrival of a newborn baby, are expected, it's essential to be cautious about pushing exhaustion to its limits. Being exhausted, in and of itself, is not inherently negative; indeed, one could argue that if you never confront exhaustion in life, you might not be working hard enough. Some individuals perceive that work-life balance equates to a perpetual lack of exhaustion, a viewpoint I disagree with. However, when exhaustion is coupled with limitations and losses, it warrants close attention, as continued exertion without periods of rest can lead to physical breakdown in various forms.

The ninth emotional response to consider is **shame.** Shame is an emotion deeply linked to one's identity. It's the sensation that something is awry with oneself, that one is insufficient, flawed, or the odd one out. The role of shame in response to limitations and losses is straightforward. When grappling with a limitation or loss and unable to effectively manage, conquer, or even adapt to it as desired, the inclination is to believe something is inherently wrong with oneself. This is where shame makes its presence felt. Shame swiftly attributes blame to your intrinsic self, highlighting your perceived inadequacies and defects. It insinuates that if you were better, you could handle the situation, but your current self falls short, hence your inability to cope. Therefore, it is crucial to exercise vigilance, self-awareness, and regulation when dealing with shame, as it tends to escalate and fixate on assigning blame in response to limitations and losses.

The tenth emotional response to limitations and losses is **fear.** Fear is an emotion influenced by proximity. It means that fear doesn't manifest until something we dread draws near, such as getting on a plane, riding an elevator, or crossing a bridge if you fear heights. Fear is a reaction to limitations and losses because many of us harbor an aversion to these circumstances. We are not the type to simply go with the flow when limitations and losses approach. Instead, we become anxious when we sense their impending arrival. When they actually manifest in our lives, our fear intensifies, often leading to a somewhat scattered response. Observing in ourselves and others the impulse to react is frequently rooted in fear. The fear revolves around the impending limitation and the potential for loss. It is crucial to recognize this, as sometimes when limitations and losses loom or are present in our lives, the appropriate response isn't to flee and hide but to remain and endure. As previously mentioned, limitations and losses follow seasonal patterns, featuring periods of turbulent storms and times when the sun shines and the weather is favorable.

The final emotional response under consideration is **guilt,** which operates on a performance-based principle. Guilt arises when we either act or fail to act. In the context of limitations and losses, guilt emerges when we falter, failing to meet our anticipated obligations or engage in actions we committed to. It entails self-reflection on the occurrence of limitations in our lives, attributing their presence to various factors. Instead of responding as we ought to, we perform actions that deviate from our expectations, subsequently internalizing a perception of personal inadequacy. Similar to shame but distinct from fear, guilt necessitates management and regulation. It must not be allowed to dominate one's inner self uncontrollably. Instead, it should be acknowledged and assessed while simultaneously restraining its influence, as guilt possesses an insatiable nature. Over time, I have asserted that parents driven by guilt find it difficult to assert the word "no" because guilt ingrains the belief that they are flawed and consequently must compensate through excessive efforts. Thus, when confronted with limitations and losses, it is permissible to acknowledge the impact and admit that our responses may have been less than ideal without the need for overcompensation. It is crucial to recognize that we are not the worst individuals in the world simply because we faced limitations and losses and may have faltered in our reactions.

I will present several strategies for you to consider adopting in order to navigate through limitations and losses in a holistic and healthy manner. The initial step you should take is to become self-aware. Enhancing your self-awareness is highly beneficial when facing limitations and losses. The reason for this is that self-awareness equips you with a deeper understanding of yourself, including your inclinations, tendencies, strengths, weaknesses, and your ability to discern when you require assistance. It grants you the knowledge of when to place trust in yourself and when to exercise caution.

An individual who possesses **self-awareness** stands a greater chance of success in navigating through seasons of limitations and losses than someone lacking this trait. The most straightforward method to cultivate self-awareness is to pose a simple question to a close, respected, and cherished individual: "What is it like to be in a relationship with me?" In clearer terms, ask about their experiences while in a relationship with you. Subsequently, when confronting a limitation or an obstacle hindering your pursuits or impeding your ability to achieve your goals, question them about your behavior and psychological and emotional responses. Inquire about your relational and spiritual demeanor during these times.

Asking questions about what occurs within our body and seeking answers to these questions is an invaluable practice. The responses from trusted and beloved individuals hold a value that surpasses that of gold. These answers will provide substantial assistance.

The second recommendation involves **recognizing and embracing** limitations and losses. While this may seem straightforward, delving deeper into this idea is necessary. Certain individuals encounter difficulty when it comes to acknowledging limitations and losses properly. Insecurity frequently leads to the perception that limitations relate to one's own inadequacies, as opposed to attributing them to external elements. Insecurity emerges when an individual holds an inflated view of others and a diminished self-value. In such situations, every circumstance tends to be interpreted as centered on the self.

Individuals who cannot recognize a limitation tend to take everything personally. When we talk about recognizing a limitation, it implies understanding that limitations and losses exist independently of you, with no personal concern for you. To illustrate, think of limitations and losses like gravity. Gravity doesn't possess personal knowledge of your identity, residence, habits, likes, or dislikes, nor does it have any intent to interfere with your life personally. Instead, gravity is a transcendent force that influences you yet remains relationally impersonal.

Understanding limitations and losses in this manner is crucial, as it prevents these concepts from becoming overly personal, emotional, or psychological. This understanding enables you to recognize that the limitations you perceive in others are not a reflection of your own limitations. It entails acknowledging their transcendent and inescapable nature as two distinct realities. Regarding the notion of embracing limitations and losses, it conveys the idea of wholeheartedly embracing them, much like an intimate embrace with kisses on the cheek, handholding, and walking together. Some may argue that this approach fosters weakness, but I disagree, and I respect those who choose to follow their own path.

I intend to convey to people that limitations and losses are two inescapable realities, and I prefer to actively engage with them. Rather than maintaining an existential relationship characterized by denial, belittlement, and pessimism, I advocate for holding the hand of limitation and loss, comprehending them, forming a connection with them, and addressing them through practical strategies. This approach is applicable in various contexts, including relationships, homes, communities, governments, organizations, businesses, and churches. In my observation, the failure to embrace limitations and losses is evident when individuals react with distress and the desire to quit as soon as these challenges arise. It has become commonplace to exclaim, "I can't take this anymore!" Yet, it is essential to recognize that the challenges one faces exist to some extent everywhere. Embracing and acknowledging limitations and losses remains one of the most effective strategies for holistically and healthily navigating through them.

The third strategy involves ***avoiding exaggerations or diminishments***. This concept has been discussed in previous writings, so it does not require an in-depth explanation. Strive to adopt a differentiated perspective when dealing with limitations and losses. Generally, limitations are neither as dire as we often perceive them to be nor as favorable as we might hope. They typically fall within a differentiated range. To be a differentiated individual means recognizing the entirety of the spectrum and all its facets simultaneously, then drawing conclusions based on the totality of these aspects. Therefore, it is essential to live in a manner that avoids both exaggeration and diminishment concerning limitations and losses.

The fourth strategy involves the ***management of expectations.*** Life's volatility often goes underestimated, akin to the stock market's concept of volatility. Just as every stock possesses a volatility index, life has its own volatility index, with limitations and losses acting as the governing factors. Hence, it becomes essential to temper our expectations. For those of us who harbor exceedingly high expectations, recognizing and accepting the influence of limitations and losses on these expectations is crucial. This doesn't necessarily imply lowering expectations but rather adjusting their pace. You can maintain high expectations, yet acknowledge that you might take longer to reach your goals due to the presence of limitations and losses. Consequently, while you may maintain high expectations, the realization that your destination might not align exactly with your initial vision should be accepted. Instead, it may be slightly higher or in a different direction due to limitations and losses. Individuals who manage their expectations amidst limitations and losses tend to experience greater happiness, fulfillment, success, relatability, and desirability in contrast to those who do not.

The fifth strategy for effectively managing limitations and losses, promoting holistic and healthy navigation, involves ***sharing them with*** *friends and loved ones.* The Bible emphasizes the concept of bearing one another's burdens, which is only achievable when people are aware of each other's struggles. This awareness hinges on the presence of vulnerability, necessitating a climate of safety. Such conditions can be realized when individuals embody qualities like humility, love, and self-awareness. The ability to swiftly apologize and adapt further contributes to creating an environment in which people can feel known and cared for. Succeeding in life is not typically a solitary endeavor, and sharing one's limitations and losses with friends and loved ones, while reciprocally assisting them with their own challenges, is essential. An individual without someone to confide in is at a disadvantage, as life was not designed to be lived in isolation. Although there are exceptional individuals who can thrive without others, this narrative does not align with the experience of most people. Success and the effective handling of limitations and losses often necessitate the support of others. I propose that one of the most efficacious ways to do this is by leaning on friends and loved ones.

The final strategy I want to emphasize is *prayer*. I understand that some readers may not be religious, and they might identify as irreligious, atheistic, or agnostic, which means this aspect may not apply to them. Nevertheless, I also recognize that a substantial portion of the global population adheres to religious beliefs and engages in prayer. In my view, prayer represents the foremost strategy for addressing limitations and losses. Prayer serves to invoke the presence and resources of the Most High God. It reminds us that we are not alone and necessitates an acknowledgment of both our capabilities and limitations. Furthermore, prayer aligns with the principles of self-awareness, aids in avoiding exaggerations and diminishments, and helps in managing expectations. It serves as a means through which we can extend assistance, express love, and support others as they navigate their own limitations and losses. In my personal life, prayer stands as my primary strategy. It is the initial action I take each morning upon waking. I address not only my own limitations and losses but also those faced by my friends and family members. I offer these concerns to the Most

High God, trusting that He will heed these prayers and, in His wisdom and according to His immeasurable resources, guide us in navigating our psychological and emotional responses to limitations and losses.

9

Chapter 9: FIVE CONCLUDING QUESTIONS

How does the complexities of our human experience factor into limitations and losses?

This discussion delves into the complexity of our human experiences and their relevance to limitations and losses. While this topic could warrant an entire book in itself, I aim to provide an overview within the scope of this chapter to align with the book's overarching purpose. Understanding limitations and losses necessitates defining and illustrating them, as well as scrutinizing their diverse components and the various effects and responses they elicit. This exploration occurs through the lens of the human experience. Despite the commonalities that unite human beings, significant differences exist among individuals. Our experiences are contingent upon our geographical location, lifestyle, the era in which we live, and can be reshaped by events, crises, pandemics, national or global limitations, and losses, as well as personal or domestic challenges.

Consequently, while we may use general terms to discuss limitations and losses, the unique nature of how each person experiences them becomes apparent when delving into the specifics. Thankfully, our shared human experience enables us to connect and offer support to one another as we navigate limitations and losses, fostering a sense of inclusivity and belonging. This collective experience gives rise to phrases like "you too," "me too," and "us too," bringing comfort during times of limitations and losses.

However, certain limitations and losses are bound to be experienced uniquely due to the complexities of our human experiences. Consider two organizations, each consisting of one hundred employees and both serving the same constituency in the same geographical region, state, and even the same zip code. These organizations may offer very similar products, differing primarily in their names and colors. Let's say that 20 percent of the employees from each company decide to leave and pursue government employment. Even though many aspects of the situation are identical, the manner in which each CEO addresses this limitation and loss may significantly differ.

The differing experiences arise from the complexity of each CEO's unique characteristics. This complexity is also what leads to variations in the way mothers respond to children who won't sleep. One mother's response may appear remarkable, while others might raise questions. These discrepancies can often be traced back to the intricacies of the human experience. Our individual predispositions, wiring, and the interplay between our nurture and nature shape how we perceive, process, and present ourselves to the world. This, in turn, contributes to the nonuniformity in how we encounter and navigate limitations and losses.

I want to emphasize that as we work through limitations and losses, it's important not to be surprised by the diversity in how individuals process these challenges.

While I believe that certain principles are universally applicable when it comes to holistic and healthy navigation through limitations and losses, the specific application of these principles can vary significantly. The duration it takes for one person to recover from a loss may differ from the time it takes another person. Additionally, one individual's ability to adapt and incorporate a limitation into their life and return to their usual pace can greatly contrast with another's, largely due to the complexities inherent in the human experience.

In addressing this issue, my aim is to create a space that accommodates individuals who may have been viewed as outliers. This space is intended for those who do not fit within the typical "us." It's meant for individuals who continue to grapple with their limitations and losses, possibly without having fully overcome them. The intent is to remind them that their journey with limitations and losses is distinctive, primarily due to the intricacies associated with the human experience.

Are there any personal benefits we can receive from limitations and losses?

Several personal benefits that can be derived from limitations and losses, although I'll only mention a few, recognizing that readers may come up with additional ones. Some readers might even have authored books or podcasts delving into this very topic, sharing what they've learned and continuing to learn from their experiences with limitations and losses. The first notable benefit is self-awareness, as few things prompt self-awareness more profoundly than encountering a limitation or experiencing a loss. Another valuable benefit is humility. As we navigate through limitations and losses, we are frequently confronted with a clearer understanding of both our strengths and limitations, gaining insight into who we are and who we are not.

In a healthy individual, these experiences typically foster humility and encourage the acknowledgment that they are a work in progress, recognizing that they are no better than anyone else. Such a disposition is a valuable one to possess. Another benefit is increased relatability. When we openly share our experiences with limitations and losses, it humanizes us in the eyes of others. They begin to perceive us as fellow humans, making us more relatable. This realization fosters the potential for deeper relationships, meaningful conversations, and the exchange of thoughts and experiences, creating a mutually beneficial connection. Additionally, limitations and losses often serve as catalysts for change, propelling individuals toward transformative growth.

As you go about your day, you typically rely on strategies that are effective until you encounter a limitation that disrupts those strategies. This necessitates the search for alternative ways to approach various aspects of life, fostering adaptability and change. While humans tend to be resistant to change, limitations and losses often serve as potent catalysts for transformation. Additionally, limitations and losses can lead to increased empathy. When we experience these challenges, we undergo emotional and psychological shifts that help us comprehend the feelings and experiences of others. This heightened empathy enables us to engage more deeply in the lives of those around us and relate to them in ways that were not possible before. These represent some of the personal benefits we can derive from limitations and losses.

How can friends help us as we face limitations and losses?

Let's discuss the ways in which friends can offer support when we encounter limitations and losses, essentially highlighting how you can assist your friends and family during such times. While I won't cover all possible ways, here are a few notable approaches. Firstly, by actively listening. Many individuals struggle with being attentive listeners, often distracted or preoccupied with their phones, failing to make meaningful eye contact. They are unable to recall or provide a concise summary of what you shared that you would confirm. To be truly helpful to someone facing limitations or losses, one must develop the skill of effective listening, much like practicing to improve one's piano-playing abilities.

To become a good listener, you'll need to practice. Assess your listening skills by asking others if they think you are a good listener. If you aspire to improve as a listener, adopt the habit of repeating back what someone has shared with you after they've finished speaking. This practice, when repeated many times, will help you acquire the skills of an effective listener. The significance of becoming a good listener lies in the fact that individuals facing limitations and losses do not have the luxury of explaining something repeatedly, expecting you to grasp it after numerous attempts.

Understanding is crucial, and if you don't comprehend something, you should ask clarifying questions until you do. One primary reason for not understanding is inadequate listening. Becoming a good listener is important because when people feel genuinely heard, they experience a sense of being loved. Another action a friend can take is to observe. This goes beyond merely looking at the person; it involves making direct eye contact and delving deeper to truly perceive the person. Take note of their habits, gestures, and mannerisms to gain a more profound understanding of the individual.

The human face often reflects our mental, emotional, spiritual, and physical condition. It's essential to develop the ability to interpret facial expressions, to perceive a person beyond their actions toward you. Look past their clothing, physical appearance, and utilitarian role. Instead, learn to observe their pain, limitations, and losses, as well as the impact these factors have on their life. Pay attention to how these experiences influence their gait, their relationships, and their professional life. Truly seeing a person is a way to make them feel loved. In our current world, people frequently feel unheard and unseen, which can lead to various forms of acting out or internalizing their struggles.

Some individuals go to great lengths to gain visibility and acknowledgment, while others withdraw and isolate themselves. Both responses, whether seeking attention or retreating, result from a perception of the world as a hostile and obscure place, which is far from ideal. To aid your friends in coping with limitations and losses, it's crucial to truly see them. Additionally, it's essential to respect the dignity of the person you wish to assist. Being asked for help is preferable to offering unsolicited aid. When you do offer help, ensure that it is genuinely helpful rather than unhelpful. Acquiring these skills is possible, but it requires a willingness to dedicate time and effort, something that many people are unwilling to do due to their preoccupation with technology and superficial matters.

Many individuals avoid the pain, challenges, and losses associated with becoming proficient at aiding others, which leads them to remain in a state of superficiality. As a result, many people are not genuinely helpful when others are experiencing limitations and losses. They may lack the knowledge of how to provide assistance effectively. To be more helpful and show respect for a person's dignity, one approach is to ask them directly, "How can I assist you?" while some may respond with, "I'm fine, you don't need to do anything," if you have truly been hearing, listening, and seeing the person, you are likely to have valuable insights on how to provide meaningful help.

Even if the person indicates that you can identify ways to assist, especially if you are not well-acquainted with them, it is advisable to seek their input. You might approach the conversation by mentioning your observations. For instance, you might say, "I've noticed that since your car accident, it's been challenging for you to carry things. How would you feel if I arrived at work early to meet you in the parking lot and help you carry your belongings?" Even if they respond with, "No, you don't have to do that," you can emphasize your willingness by saying, "I know I don't have to do that, but I want to." This approach respects the person's dignity and obtains their permission to offer assistance. This way, you are helping the person while preserving their dignity.

Friends are not meant to be saviors but companions, considering that we, too, encounter limitations and losses in our lives. Additionally, a friend's presence is invaluable when they are physically there. Despite the convenience of phones and technology, they can never substitute the profound impact of being physically present with someone. The sensory experiences, from scents to touch and ambiance, bring something unique and irreplaceable. The essence of another person's physical presence is extraordinary and unparalleled, making it one of the most meaningful acts of support one can offer to another.

In times of limitation and loss, it's crucial to be as present as possible. In addition to being present, you must believe in the individual. This means looking into their eyes and expressing your belief in them, your love for them, and your trust in their abilities. They need to hear your encouragement, such as "You can do this, and I'm here to help." Just like athletes have fans in the stands, everyone requires unwavering support from someone who genuinely believes in them. You should be a consistent, loyal friend who is physically present and unwaveringly believes in the person facing limitations and losses. By incorporating these four elements into friendships, you can provide substantial assistance to those in need.

When should we get help with them?

This question is essential, as I'm genuinely concerned about people and their well-being. I would love for everyone to live in a world where they feel acknowledged, heard, and supported by others who believe in them. It's important for people to know they are not alone and can receive the help they need when facing limitations and losses. There are specific situations when seeking help becomes imperative for those experiencing limitations and losses. In such circumstances, waiting, hoping, or praying for assistance may not be enough; one must actively seek help. Here are a few scenarios to consider.

If you find yourself contemplating taking your own life in response to a limitation or loss, it's crucial to seek help. I understand that many individuals hesitate to do so due to the fear of judgment, condemnation, or the prospect of being admitted to a hospital. However, I strongly believe that you should reach out for assistance. Numerous resources are available, including the National Suicide Hotline, counseling services, and trusted friends and loved ones who won't overreact and will support you during this difficult time.

In the case that you suddenly become involved in extreme activities with the intention of self-sabotage, hoping for a tragic outcome, or if you find yourself engaging in dangerous pursuits as a response to limitations and losses, it is essential to seek help. Another scenario that warrants seeking help is when you consistently experience strong emotional and psychological responses that significantly disrupt your daily life. If feelings of frustration, anger, pessimism, and hopelessness have reached a point where they interfere with your sleep, appetite, relationships, and work performance, it is crucial to get help. These are three situations where seeking help is strongly recommended.

Where is God at in all of this?

The question arises: Where is God in the context of limitations and losses? Earlier in this book, it was mentioned that, for some individuals, the presence of limitations and losses serves as an argument against the existence of God. They perceive the universe as a tumultuous, dark, and perilous place. The myriad instances of limitations and losses, including death, war, evil, and celestial phenomena, make it challenging for them to reconcile such a reality with the existence of a divine being. They question the purpose of it all and whether a divine being who permits limitations and losses is desirable. While I can empathize with this perspective to some extent, I do not share the same viewpoint. The question remains: Where is God in all of this?

It is my belief that God is in close proximity to those who have broken hearts, and His presence is most profound for those who endure the deepest suffering caused by limitations and losses. Sometimes, our search for God takes us to the wrong places. We tend to presume that God resides in paradisiacal settings, under the radiant sun, on pristine beaches, in luxurious locations like Dubai or penthouse suites atop towering buildings. We often assume that God is associated with good health, happiness, pleasure, birth, scholastic and athletic achievements, and remarkable accomplishments. Blessings and gratitude toward God come easily when we experience positive events. However, we tend to overlook God's presence in the midst of limitations and losses.

Within the context of the Christian and biblical perspective, I propose that God is the deity of limitations and losses. To encounter Him and experience His presence more profoundly, one should look to periods characterized by limitations and losses. In the Bible's narrative, the darkest chapters in human history often contain the most profound manifestations of God's presence. These are the moments when God tends to reveal Himself most prominently. Throughout what I would refer to as redemptive history, this pattern repeats itself.

For those who are currently grappling with limitations or losses and find themselves pondering the question, "Where is God?" It's essential to recognize that God's presence is closer than one might initially perceive. When we face the loss of people and things or live within the confines of limitations, our perception often skews towards malevolence over benevolence. We tend to view all limitations and losses as negative, although some are undeniably more severe than others. These limitations and losses represent an overarching reality in our current age, but they are not everlasting. Amidst these struggles, we are recipients of divine and human assistance, supported by both promises and real-life experiences.

I consider faith to hold genuine value when it functions effectively during our most challenging moments. On the other hand, religion serves no purpose if it fails to provide guidance and support in our direst times. A God who remains absent in the face of limitations and losses, not necessarily to rescue us from them but unquestionably to help us navigate through them in diverse ways, cannot be considered a true God.

Nevertheless, I firmly believe that God manifests in our moments of limitations and losses. He is undeniably present amidst them. One of our primary difficulties lies in our expectation of encountering Him in a superhuman or miracle-working guise. We anticipate Him to appear in the form of a savior, always providing immediate deliverance.

However, there are times when He is simply present to sit with us in silent companionship or to observe from a distance, but His presence is unwavering.

In certain instances, I must admit my profound empathy for individuals. Despite my unwavering religious convictions, I occasionally find myself inclined to approach God and present the following argument: "These people struggle to believe in you because they cannot perceive your presence. I have faith in your existence, yet they cannot sense you or experience your assistance during their times of limitations and losses. Consequently, their belief in you falters. For those who do believe, they may perceive you as a malevolent rather than a benevolent God because they perceive you as a passive observer of their suffering, taking no action." Some of my contemporaries may respond by asserting that my approach toward God is disrespectful.

However, I maintain my belief that God possesses the capacity to comprehend my intentions, and my approach is not a condemnation of Him. It signifies the point where my human wisdom reaches its limit. I do not approach God with fear and trembling but rather as a compassionate being who understands my human weaknesses and vulnerabilities. My approach is one of seeking understanding, compassion, and empathy, not adversarial in nature. I seek to comprehend the plight of those enduring limitations and losses and to bring their struggles to God's attention, however futile that may be. So, if you currently find yourself in a situation of limitation and loss and you're pondering the whereabouts of God, I assure you that it is a valid question to ask.

Chapter 10: DISCUSSION QUESTIONS

Prior to reading this book, had you ever heard of limitations and losses?

____

____

____

____

____

____

What stands out to you the most about them?

____

____

____

____

____

____

If you had to define them using your own words, how would you do that?

____

____

____

____

____

____

What are they doing in you and to you?

____

____

____

____

____

____

What emotions and thoughts, in you, are most associated with them?

____

____

____

____

____

____

What is your biggest challenge with them?

How do you see them at work in the world and how do you see them being addressed?

From your perspective, what are some of the most common ways people deal with them?

How do you see them at work in the workplace and how are they typically addressed?

____

____

____

____

____

____

How do you see them at work in the family and how are they typically addressed?

____

____

____

____

____

____

ABOUT THE AUTHOR

Michael is a serial intellectual. He creates intellectual products that transform people and change the world. He was born in Los Angeles and lived there for almost four decades. In 2009, he moved to Baltimore City and has lived there for fourteen years. Michael has five beautiful adult children. Michael has a bachelor's degree in political studies with an emphasis in philosophy as well as a master's degree in divinity.

He is a certified Enneagram administrator, Scrum master and trained in project management. Michael has been coaching and consulting for twenty-five years. He has founded and led multiple nonprofit organizations. Michael is the author of ten books; *100 Meditations: An Everyday Book for Everyday People; Don't Plant, Be Planted; Metamorphic Dictis; Be You; Social Revolution is Baltimore's Only Solution; Hard Questions*, Tenses, Emotional Triumvirate and Differentiated. Michael is also the creator of the eight personal development tools: Pause exercise, Emotional MRI, How to Write Strategic Affirmations, Life Map, Pillars of Personal Development, Priority Funnel, Quadroscope and Mirror Exercise.

Michael is an accomplished triathlete and has completed all four distances. Michael's favorite sport is motocross, his favorite fast food is In-N-Out Burger, he is addicted to fresh Reese's Peanut Butter Cups, and absolutely loves rottweilers. His favorite animals are killer whales and tigers. One of his favorite authors is Mark Twain, and one of his favorite quotes from him is "The two most important days of your life are the day you are born and the day you find out why.”

www.ingramcontent.com/pod-product-compliance
Lightning Source LLC
Chambersburg PA
CBHW052115150726
48002CB00006B/2352